LEPROSY IN THE CHURCH

Marcia A. Morrison

Leprosy In The Church
by Marcia Morrison

Printed in the United States of America

ISBN 1-594677-23-9

www.xulonpress.com

I dedicate this book
in memory of my late husband

~ Minstrel Seth Jonathan Morrison ~

whose heartfelt love, inspiration, friendship
and covering over my life will always be
reminisced like a fresh summer breeze

You were my "coach in the corner"
and I will forever be grateful to God for your
abbreviated, yet powerful life

~ TABLE OF CONTENTS ~

~ ACKNOWLEDGMENTS ~

My deepest appreciation is extended to:

- ❖ My two very patient daughters Chauncey Ciera Rayford and Mikailah Star Morrison. My gems of inspiration, you are the two most precious children any mother could have. You are my angels sent from God, and you make me smile. Unselfishly, you lend me to the Body of Christ, and I could not have completed this book without your understanding. I truly cherish the blessing you are in my life and love each of you deeply.
- ❖ My parents Suffragan Bishop Lawrence E. Brown, Sr. and First Lady Kate T. Brown. You are absolutely the greatest parents in the world and I love you dearly! You have stood by my side, rejoicing with me through the mountain-top experiences and encouraging me through the valleys. Words can not express how much I appreciate having you in my life as you are my candid advisors, my strongest supporters, and my best friends.
- ❖ My spiritual mother and mentor Dr. Juanita Bynum. From the first day I encountered you, your love, support, and life at large have simply amazed me! I have received multiple impartations from God through your hands and the prophetic flow from your lips which have helped usher me to this accomplishment.

I know no one in the universe more transparent, generous of heart or thirsty for God than you.

❖ My spiritual covering Bishop George & Lady Mary Searight. A prince and a very fair lady - you are two of the most precious, loving, and caring shepherds one can ever find in the Lord's kingdom. Your prayer support, encouragement, and understanding of the call on my life have meant more than you will ever know. I love and appreciate you both.

❖ My adjutant Karen Michelle Christie. From the first day you came to me years ago and said, "God told me to follow you," you have been right by my side through all the ministry transitions and were first partaker and reader of this book. I greatly appreciate your diligence and love for the Lord and His work.

❖ My ministry help, the Morrison Ministries team. Karla "Vikki" Christie, Barbara "Pie" Dixon, Tracy Hamilton, and Lashay Johnson - you are among the hardest working, most faithful girls I know and are the feet that help walk out this work.

❖ My siblings in the Lord John and CeeCee Miller. John you are one of the hardest working men in the world. Thank you for your untiring labor to make this book a reality.

~ FOREWORD ~

*I*t's time to take your spiritual pulse…because God is calling His Bride to holiness. Like never before. The words Paul spoke in Ephesians 5:25–27 were prophetic of a deadly condition in the Church today, "Husbands, love your wives, as Christ loved the church and gave Himself up for her. So that He might sanctify her, having cleansed her by the washing of water with the Word. That He might present the church to Himself in glorious splendor, without spot or wrinkle or any such things [that she might be holy and faultless]" (Ampl.).

In other words, God knew the Church would be sick. He knew we would have spots, blemishes, wrinkles, and faults that needed to be washed away. And He foreknew that a season of purging and cleansing would come before He returns to the earth with a mighty deliverance.

Hear me. Pay special attention to the words of my spiritual daughter, Marcia. I am convinced she has heard the Word of the Lord. More than this, *I know her.* She's a true servant of God. Over the past several years, I have been blessed to serve as her mentor and have witnessed God's hand in her life. She's real…and she's a broken vessel. Marcia has humbled herself before God, and He's raising her up with an anointed message that should be preached from every pulpit.

Don't see the word, "leprosy," and run from this message. That's been humanity's problem from the beginning. You see, when a person has leprosy, he doesn't want to look in the mirror...*which hides the problem from the one who needs to see it most.* He might feel better by turning away from the issue, but in reality, his condition is only getting worse. Leprosy eats away at your relationship with God *and* with other people. When this happens, the devil couldn't be happier.

Jesus made people identify their issues. And when they did, He healed them *according to their faith.* Don't run away from this message. God has given Marcia "calculated measures" to identify the disease that can paralyze you, isolate you, and make you ineffective for God. And she doesn't stop there. She gives *spiritual medicine* straight from the Word of God that can build your faith, so that you can believe Him to heal areas of your heart that have always been "untouchable."

Listen to me. Don't reject the cleansing. *Embrace it—* because without the cleansing, you'll never be healed. Without the cleansing, you can't be presented to Jesus "without spot or wrinkle..." Without the cleansing, God's people can never become one and the world won't be able to see who Jesus really is (see John 17).

Hear a prophetic voice that's crying out for the Church to prepare for her Groom's return. And then...*listen to your heartbeat.*

Dr. Juanita Bynum

~ INTRODUCTION ~

The Plague of Leprosy

"When the plague of leprosy is in a man..."
Leviticus 13:9

Many are asking themselves, "What is wrong with the church?" Essentially everywhere you look there exists a deep-seated, prevailing problem across the Body of Christ. Although our ministries are larger than they have ever been in history, there is still something awry in Christendom. We have been trying to define what it is that has gripped the church at large, but can not quite put our finger on it to accurately diagnose this condition. The mass majority has grown weary of what seems to be an epidemic in the Body of Christ that has spread extensively. From pastors to prophets to evangelists to choir members to ushers to pew members - from the pulpit to the pews every part of the Body has a touch of this thing. It has no respect of persons or position. Even the unsaved recognize it to the point where many of them claim not to want to come to our churches because of it. Chances are that if you as a believer have not noticed that something severe has hit the church and that we need serious help from God, then you may be among those inflicted by this contagion. If you think that the church at large is okay in its current condition and does not need a true change, then it is very likely that this spiritual epidemic has affected you as well. So the question becomes this: What is this thing that has heavily engrossed the church? What is truly wrong with the church?

It is called "leprosy."

One day I was lying across my bed studying the Word of God and the Lord spoke to me and said, "Marcia, the Body is leprous." Bewildered and puzzled by what I knew was clearly the voice of God that had just spoken, I was anxious to understand what the Spirit of the Lord was trying to communicate to me. The words that I heard God speak sat upon my heart and so captured my attention that I briefly paused and before I knew it, I heard my audible voice quickly responding to God and asking, "Lord, what do you mean?" You see there are those moments in your walk with God that you know that you have just had an encounter with the Master that has an assignment attached to it. As you grow in the Spirit, you come to the place where you recognize that when God opens you up to divine illumination and brings a message to you, it is not to tickle you, impress you or to make you go, "Wow!" It is, however, to incite you and enlist you into your next kingdom assignment. This was one of those sobering moments wherein it was clear that a mandate of some sort had just stepped up on me because God never reveals anything to His servants without requiring an act of obedience afterwards. His illumination always comes laced with an instruction that must be carried out for the sake of the Body of Christ.

Immediately after I had asked God what He meant when He spoke to me and said that "...the Body is leprous," the Spirit of the Lord led me to Leviticus 13:9 - 15 as the basis for what He said and to reveal His heart because everything that God speaks is always rooted in His Word. Here begins the reading of the Word of the Lord found in Leviticus 13:9 - 15:

When the plague of leprosy is in a man, then he shall be brought unto the priest; And the priest shall see him: and, behold, if the rising be white in the skin, and it have turned the hair white, and there be quick raw flesh in the rising; It is an old leprosy in the skin of his flesh, and the priest shall pronounce him unclean, and shall not shut him up: for he is unclean. And if a leprosy break out abroad in the skin, and the leprosy cover all the skin of him that hath the plague from his head even to his foot, wheresoever the priest looketh; Then the priest shall consider: and, behold, if the leprosy have covered all his flesh, he shall pronounce him clean that hath the plague: it is all turned white: he is clean. But when raw flesh appeareth in him, he shall be unclean. And the priest shall see the raw flesh, and pronounce him to be unclean: for the raw flesh is unclean: it is a leprosy.

I was awestruck as I read this Word of the Lord because it seemed as though the letter of the Word leaped from the pages and stood up boldly in my face as if to confront me with a serious issue. I felt arrested, I felt charged with a crime, and I felt responsible to do something about this indictment, this heavy charge that God was bringing against the church of my generation at large. He began to open up to me in fine detail the diagnosis of this epidemic, this plague that has infiltrated the Body of Christ. The Lord unveiled to me the different symptoms of spiritual leprosy that are prevalent within Christendom. As is done when we go to the doctor for a physical exam or check up on our natural bodies to determine how healthy we are, it was as if God, the Great Physician (Jeremiah 8:22), was performing a spiritual check up on the Body of Christ, highlighting the various symptoms that diagnose our condition to be leprous.

When was the last time you had a physical checkup to determine how physically healthy you are? Do you remember your most recent heart exam or the last time your eyes were checked to determine the clarity of your vision? How about your heart rate? What are your pulse and the nominal pressure of your blood that flows through your heart? In other words, what is your blood pressure? Are your kidneys functioning fine? What about your liver? How do you know that you are living free of disease and infirmity? According to the American Medical Association, one should have a physical exam at least once per year as a maintenance check. However, many do not follow that medical advice which is why statistics report that the majority of sicknesses that occur could have been avoided by early detection through physical checkups or by lifestyle adjustments in advance.

As it is in the natural, so it is in the spirit. When was the last time you had a spiritual check up? How do you know how well you are spiritually and what your level is in God? How can you be sure that you are not inflicted with sin sickness, even though you have been saved for years and may be serving in high office as a prophet, evangelist, pastor, etc.? Like cancer, the sin of leprosy creeps up on a healthy body without you knowing it until it gets to the point of destruction. Unfortunately, many of us have never even fathomed the concept or thought of having a spiritual checkup conducted on us. Therefore, most of us have no clue whether or not spiritual infirmity has set up in our hearts. Have you ever checked your spiritual heart to ensure that it beats with the rhythm of the life of God? What is your spiritual pulse, and how active is the blood of Jesus in your life? Is your father's DNA detected in your blood which causes you to live and act like Him? What about your inner eyes - can you see in the Spirit or are you spiritually blind or have spiritual cataracts? What about your hearing? Are your ears clogged or are you spiritually deaf to the point that you can not hear a Word

Leprosy In The Church

from the Lord? Are your feet crippled like Mephibosheth (2 Samuel 4:4), causing you not to be able to walk upright before God? Is your reproductive system alive or do you have dry breasts and a miscarrying womb? (Hosea 9:14) Are you so immature in the Spirit that you can not eat meat because you have for years been at baby stage and your system can not handle strong meat? Does meat choke you, keeping you on the milk of the Word? (Hebrews 5:12 - 14) Do you have hair, denoting the glory of God on your life or have you gone bald at a young age? (Ezekiel 7:18) How do you know that you are not inflicted with the plague of leprosy? Simply put, the Body of Christ is far overdue to be examined via spiritual checkup and for treatment by the Word.

The 21ˢᵗ century church in its current state is infirmed and is in much need of a physician. The prophet Jeremiah asks the question, "Is there no Balm in Gilead; is there no Physician there? why then is not the health of the daughter of my people recovered?" (Jeremiah 8:22) Jeremiah is posing the question to the people of God and saying in other words, "Isn't there a cure for our condition? Isn't there a Physician among us capable of diagnosing and treating our spiritual infirmity? Isn't there a remedy for us so that we don't have to remain the way we are?" The answer is, undoubtedly, yes! There is help for the people of God; there is indeed a Balm in Gilead that can not only diagnose our condition, but more importantly, His Word is also the medicine to cure and heal what ails the Body. There is indeed help for wicked evangelists, a way out for lying prophets, a cure for fornicating musicians, etc. In fact, the Father has sent this book as an emergency kit to jump-start the heart of the church to help (along with other co-laborers) to get the Body of Christ back on track with God.

I recommend highly that through this book you allow the Physician that Jeremiah speaks of to examine your spirit. David said, "Examine me, O Lord, and prove me; try my reins and my heart." (Psalm 26:3) Then Paul says, "Examine yourselves, whether ye be in the faith..." (2 Corinthians 13:5) The Word of God is the yardstick by which we assess and diagnose ourselves - not by which we compare ourselves to others. (2 Corinthians 10:13) It is the stethoscope to monitor our own heartbeat. It performs an X-ray, MRI, and CAT scan on our inner man to uncover the hidden things that we tend to gloss over, either through ignorance or simply pretending that they do not exist. On the other hand, some of us have harbored conditions in our natural bodies that we did not know existed until we got a check up. It is then that the doctor reveals our condition and may have to begin aggressive treatment based on the severity of the disease and its progression. Again, as it is in the natural, so it is in the spirit. There are unrevealed issues that many of us contend with that need to be uncovered and dealt with, even when we may not be aware of their existence and detriment. Cancer is just as harmful to the body whether you know you have it or not.

Allow me to testify. While writing this book, the Spirit of the Lord also examined me for leprosy, and His diagnosis revealed some areas in my own life that I needed God to cleanse me from. By the human nature of the flesh, your first inclination is to deny what God is showing you and claim, "That's not me!" His Word then shines the light on your condition again and says affirmatively, "Look! See! That is you!" How is it that we attempt to tell God that He is wrong when He calls out our mess?! Romans 3:4 says, "God forbid: yea, let God be true, but every man a liar." When God shows you your shortcomings, if within your mind you begin to rationalize why you do what you do and why you are the way you are, then it is almost certain that the Word has found you where you are and has uncovered a leprous area in your life. Do not reject this cleansing because it will be good for you. Get ready for a good ol' fashioned spiritual bath that will clean you up and prepare you for greatness in God. I had to take a good Holy Ghost look at my own self because, when it is all said and done, this thing is between me and God, which paralyzes me from being able to point a finger at anyone else but myself. I want to be right with God, I want to be purified, and I want to be holy; and there are some other blood-washed believers who also hunger for holiness and righteousness and are on a hunt to embrace it at any cost. The serious seekers have set out on a God-chase to find Him and to be conformed like Him even if it takes the death of our flesh. These are those who have come to the point where there is no more compromising or comparing ourselves with others, but we endeavor to be compared to and measured up against the Word of God alone which is the true reed and rod that John speaks of in Revelation 11:1 - 2.

The Lord specifically told Moses how to determine if the plague of leprosy was in the camp among the children of Israel. Because it was such a debilitating and crippling disease, there was much attention given to diagnosing and cleansing leprosy. Rarely is as much focus and extensive detailed instruction given to a subject as is given to leprosy in Leviticus chapters 13 and 14. This implies that God intended for His people to be keenly aware of the dangers of this plague. Sadly enough, though, it seems that whenever God places emphasis on a thing, we seem to ignore the voice of the Spirit with the ungodly assumption that God's Word is like some fairy tale that is really not true and should not be taken seriously. Just as there are key symptoms that indicate when a person has the flu (e.g. fever, coughing, nausea, wheezing, fatigue, etc.), there are also key symptoms that indicate when a person is inflicted with spiritual leprosy. *"Leprosy In The Church"* breaks down for us many of the signs that identify that leprosy has set up in the Body of Christ.

God has provided for us in this book a set of what I call "truth symptoms" that can tell you based on the truth of the

Word of God whether or not you, your ministry, or your church have been inflicted by the spirit of leprosy. These indicators are called "truth symptoms" because they come directly from the Word of truth and are not based on man's opinions, presumptions, or logic. They are straight out of the mouth of God through His Word and are intended to expose the truth. Jesus said in John 17:17 in His intercessory prayer for the disciples, "Sanctify them through Thy truth: Thy Word is Truth." It is high time for the Body of Christ to begin to see ourselves the way we really are - the way God sees us according to the measure of the Truth of God's Word. No more false prophesies and lying flattery that causes our condition to grow worse. We need to take a good, long look into the mirror of the Word and admit our short-comings and our sin which is the first step to true deliverance and revival. For instance, if you are a liar, humble yourself, admit you are a liar and get set free. The Spirit of the Lord is calling for the church to repent.

Although there are several principles that can be extracted from the Word of God regarding the plague of leprosy, the focus here is limited to eight prevailing Biblical "truth symptoms" of leprosy that shed powerful, revealing light not only on the condition of the church today but also on the prophetic direction God is taking the Body of Christ at large. As you read the upcoming eight symptoms of leprosy, open your heart, be candid and real with yourself, and embrace the conviction of the Lord that is sure to come. Because a mighty wind of revival is about to sweep the world, the Lord is cleaning us up and getting us ready for a great move of God that will usher in the return of our Lord and Savior Jesus Christ.

The Spirit of the Lord bids the church to come out of the dark and turn the light on! As you read this book, the Holy Ghost of God is going to quicken your spirit and the light of the Word is going to illuminate in your heart in a way that you may have never experienced before. If you have been walking in darkness - in the church or otherwise - then get ready because you are coming out of darkness and your spirit is going to embrace the light. There is a treatment in the medical community called "light therapy" that uses light as a type of medicine to treat illnesses in the same way as other medicines taken by mouth. Well, consider the Word of the Lord in this book your light therapy that is going to shine the light of the Word on your heart, driving out confusion and darkness and identifying the leprous areas in your life. (John 8:12) Specifically, at the end of this book, there is a measure developed out of the Word of God by which you will be able to conduct your own personal Spiritual Wellness Check to generally assess the condition of your spirit and that will highlight for you how healthy you are in God. Get ready to go on a journey that is sure to give you a belly washing that will transform you toward sanctification, righteousness, holiness, and purification. As you receive the Word of the Lord delivered in this book and ingest the Manna on these pages, you are guaranteed by the Holy Spirit to experience a divine breakthrough that will change your life, church and ministry forever.

Chapter 1

Quick Raw Flesh

Truth Symptom #1:
~ Leprosy exposes quick raw flesh ~

"When the plague of leprosy is in a man…and the priest shall see him…and if there be quick raw flesh in the rising…it is an old leprosy…"
Leviticus 13:9 - 11

*L*epers had spots of exposed flesh on their bodies. One key indicator that determines whether or not you, your church or your ministry is inflicted with the spirit of leprosy is when there is *quick raw flesh in the rising*. The word *quick* translates from the Hebrew word *michyah* which means live, preserved or sustained alive. The term *raw* comes from the Hebrew word *chay* which means to be strong, to be alive, or to be fresh. So in essence, leprosy exists when there is boastful, strong, live, fresh flesh exposed. Outside of the devil himself, your flesh is your greatest, most dangerous enemy and is also a chief enemy of God. Paul says in Romans 7:18a, "For I know that in me (that is in my flesh,) dwelleth no good thing…" and that the flesh or carnality is a staunch enemy of God (Romans 8:7). Given that all this is true, then why do we trust our flesh? It leads us wrong every time and is inherently encoded to war against the Holy Spirit within you. The works of the flesh are so strong and resistant that it takes the divine power of God to kill the flesh while you still live in it as an earthly tabernacle, temple, or house. Scripture declares in 2 Corinthians 5:1,

> For we know that if our earthly house of this tabernacle were dissolved, we have a building of God, a house not made with hands, eternal in the heavens.

Living in these bodies which are fleshly, earthen vessels (2 Corinthians 4:7) makes us co-habitants with the enemy of our souls and of God. This means that we sleep with this enemy, walk with this enemy, eat with this enemy, and even go to church with this enemy. You take this enemy everywhere you go and it is present at everything you do. Paul explains it well when he says, "I find then a law, that, when I would do good, evil is always present with me." (Romans 7:21) The flesh, however, is not a silent co-habitant or house mate; but it is a loud, proud, boastful murderer that has every intention of standing up strong in you in order to take over your life, lead you to destruction, and separate you from God.

If you are a born again believer, then not only do you live or dwell in an earthen, fleshly vessel, but the Holy Spirit has also taken up residence and dwells in you. Now you got real trouble because you have two staunch enemies (the flesh against the Holy Spirit) living in the same dwelling place. In fact, the Bible says in 1 Corinthians 6:19, "What? Know ye not that your body is the temple of the Holy Ghost which is in you, which ye have of God, and ye are not your own?"

So, in essence, as James 4:1 affirms, you have a major war going on in your members. There is a blood battle between your will and the will of God, between your flesh and the Spirit of God; and your human spirit is caught in the middle. There is something always tugging at me, trying to pull me away from God and into uncleanness. And when I surrender to this tug on me, I feel contaminated by this thing. I feel that there is something I have to get off of me and cleansed from so that I can get back in my place with God. What is this uncleanness that I feel when I let sin have its way? Well, the apostles Paul and Peter make mention of this thing that plagues me when I yield to sin. Paul says, in Ephesians 5:27,

> That He [Jesus] might present it to Himself a glorious church, not having **spot,** or wrinkle, or any such thing; but that it should be holy and without **blemish**.

Then Peter says in 2 Peter 3:14,

> Wherefore, beloved...be diligent that ye may be found of Him in peace, without **spot**, and blameless.

He also states in 2 Peter 2:13 - 15,

> And shall receive the reward of unrighteousness, as they that count it pleasure to riot in the day time. **Spots** they are and **blemishes**, sporting themselves with their own deceivings while they feast with you; having eyes full of adultery and that cannot cease from sin; beguiling unstable souls: a heart they have exercised with covetous practices; cursed children: which have forsaken the right way and are gone astray...

So, what are these spots? Are they like freckles that come on your natural body? What are these blemishes? What does it mean spiritually to have a spot or a blemish? Well, as we yield to and indulge in carnality and the things of the flesh, Jude 23 says that we then become "spotted by the flesh." Our spirit man becomes contaminated and blemished by our fleshly ways. According to 2 Peter 2:13- 15 above, we can get so far from God in unrighteousness to the point where we become labeled as spots and blemishes - just plain old, walking flesh void of the Spirit of God operating in our lives. And this can happen right in the church. This can take place while you are still evangelizing, still prophesying, still singing in the choir, still ushering, still pastoring, etc. Peter further speaks of how those that are spots and blemishes get caught up in their own deception, deceiving themselves to believe a lie and not the truth right while they feast, fellowship and worship among the righteous in the church. Deception, adultery, guile, covetousness, forsaking righteousness - these are all mentioned by Peter as spots and blemishes that breed the spirit of leprosy in the church.

Peter strongly refers to those spotted by the flesh as "sporting themselves with their own deceivings." The term *sport* comes from the Greek term *entruphao* which means to revel in, to take great pleasure or delight in, to make merry while engaging in uproarious festivities, or to make noisy festivities. Therefore, if I sport myself according to the scripture, then I take great delight and pleasure in my own self, my own ministry, my own calling, my own anointing, my own vision, my own dream, my own program, my own auxiliary, etc. always making a noisy uproar to celebrate myself - when in fact I am really deceived. My, my, my...me, me, me...I, I, I. The Body of Christ is chalk full of "I." "I" is a one letter word that can spell F-L-E-S-H; and too much "I" can lead to a great downfall. Let Lucifer testify of this. He got caught up in his own will where he constantly stated "I" will (Isaiah 14:12 - 23) which led to his ultimate downfall and destruction. All the hoopla we make over ourselves is wrapped in the enemy's lies and trickery to lead to your own demise while deceiving you to believe that you are more than what you really are and that you are not really as bad as the scriptures say you are.

The popularity of the church has drawn millions to claim themselves to be Christian or saved. There has been a major increase in church membership on roll, but not all these church members are born-again, blood bought believers. Just like a natural family where you must become a member either by being born in, adopted in, or through marriage, you must likewise become a true member of the family of God by spiritual birth (John 3:1 - 8), by spiritual adoption (Ephesians 1:5), or by spiritual marriage (Ephesians 5:21 - 33, Revelation 19:7 - 9). God has never changed His Word. Bypassing the altar of repentance and salvation and shaking the preacher's hand does not make you right with God. It makes you right with the pastor, but not with God. What has happened to the church is that among the massive influx of people that have come into the church are the many that have come running towards the glamour of church hype and sensationalism which is at an all-time high. Many have been drawn because the prophetic has now become a glamorous alternative to the psychic network. We want our spiritual palms read by the prophet so that we can know our future. Some are so spotted by the flesh that they even make you pay for prophesy because they know how desperate you are for an answer (false or otherwise) to your problems and that you do not have the Word of God hidden in your heart which enables you to discern the enemy and not be deceived.

The enemy has launched much deception in the 21st century church. The passage in 2 Peter 2:13 - 15 also describes those spotted and blemished by fleshly unrighteousness as ones who beguile unstable souls. These are those that intentionally and cunningly manipulate and deceive those that do not have a strong foundation in God. Unstable souls are those that really do not know the Word of God and are teetering and unbalanced in their walk with God. The church is full of unstable people who lack a strong grounding in the

Lord and who are looking for something that will deliver them from the everyday problems of life that weigh them down. Because they are unstable and lack the knowledge of the Word, then they can not discern when a false prophet or lying evangelist that is full of leprosy is ministering to them.

The spirit of leprosy has quick raw flesh exposed in numerous ways in the Body of Christ. Not only has it caused prophelying and other manifestations of raw flesh on parade, but it has created a frenzy in the area of the laying on of hands and falling out under the power of God. Have you noticed that everywhere you look, people are anxious to lay hands? That is because it has become a popular, glamorous, self-exalting thing to do in the church. We lay hands on people with the intention of proving that people "fall out under the power of God" when we minister. And when people do fall out when we lay hands on them, we make a noisy uproar to draw attention to ourselves as if it were our own power at work and as if this makes us great. God declares in Zechariah 4:6 that it is "...Not by [human] might, nor by [human] power, but by My Spirit saith the Lord of hosts." Let me announce to you that everybody that falls out when hands are laid on them are not falling out under the true power of God. This "falling out" craze has become a fad in the church, and many people are convinced that this is what is expected of you to prove that you have received something from God when this is not the case at all. You can receive more from the true Spirit of God standing up than you can by falling down under false pretense. Furthermore, a lot of preachers who are caught up in their own side show and circus will push you down if you do not fall down on your own. Have you ever had this to happen to you? I have, and it was quite ridiculous. In fact, in one instance, I was preaching for a bishop's banquet and after ministering, the bishop's wife came over to embrace and lay hands on me to restore virtue. When she recognized during her praying for me that I was not about to fall out, she literally wrestled me down to the floor to force me to "fall out in the Spirit." Quick raw flesh had deceived her to believe that causing Evang. Morrison to fall out under the power of God would be a powerful display to the people of the anointing on her own life. How ridiculous! So to prevent embarrassment and stop the wrestling (because she was not going to), I just gave her a "courtesy fall" to get it over with. The people were indeed impressed with her at this point, and she walked away happy to have been able to expose her power. Just like in my case, there are many, many "courtesy falls" granted in our church services, and everybody falling out is not being moved by the Holy Ghost.

Let me explain to you that the reason people truly go out under the hand of God is because the true glory of the Lord is so powerful that it consumes my spirit to the point that I experience the physical manifestation of His power. My body or flesh becomes so overwhelmed by the authentic glory of God that its strength decreases and becomes weakened. This is when I then fall out under the power of God and is why we will need glorified bodies in heaven because our physical bodies in their current, corruptible state can not stand under the raw power and glory of God. (1 Corinthians 15:53, 54) When John was caught up in the Spirit on the Lord's day in Revelation 1:10, 17 the Bible says that when he encountered the presence of the Lord, "he fell at His feet as dead." When Daniel experienced a mighty visitation from the Spirit of God, the scripture says the following in Daniel 10:8, 9, 15,

> Therefore I was left alone, and saw this great
> vision, and there remained no strength in me: for
> my comeliness was turned in me into corruption,
> and I retained no strength. Yet I heard the voice of
> His words: and when I heard the voice of His

word, then I was in a deep sleep on my face, and
my face toward the ground…And when He had
spoken such words unto me, I set my face toward
the ground, and became dumb.

Falling out under the power of God always comes with
a purpose. It is like being under spiritual anesthetic. Both
John and Daniel received major revelation and impartation
from God while the Holy Spirit caused them to be slain
under His power. Whenever you experience the intense
glory of God to the point of going out under the Spirit, the
Lord is conducting surgery on you, doing an operation to
either deposit something in you (righteousness) or to cut
something away from you (flesh). The key focus is not my
falling out, but it is on what happens to me while I am out
under the power of God and how I come out from under that
divine visitation. Falling out in the Spirit is not just for sport
or for show. Jesus said in John 3:30 regarding the Father's
work in Him, "He must increase, but I must decrease."
When my flesh decreases then the Spirit of God increases
and can work and operate on, through, and in me. You must
therefore ask yourself if or when you go out under God's
true glory, "What was God doing in me? What did the Lord
just pluck out of my spirit? What seed did He just deposit in
my belly? What vision did God just give me? How am I different as a result of my laying out prostrate before God? "
You see, I can fall out all I want, but if I rise up still evil,
covetous, jealous, competitive, greedy, a liar, and with no
vision or direction, then my falling out was fleshly and in
vain, meant absolutely nothing, and was a wasted sport.

If you are a man or woman of God that practices push-
ing people down to prove that the power of God is resting on
you, then it may very well be the case that you are in fact
powerless and therefore feel that you have to exert your own
physical strength to get a fleshly manifestation that will

draw attention to you. This is a symptom of the quick, raw flesh caused by leprosy. Further, do not get caught up in the fact that people fall out when you pray for or lay hands on them. Do you not know that the enemy is tricking us to get so caught up in the hype and euphoria of "churchism" and religious fads that we miss the true glory of God? If people can get emotional to the point of fainting and falling out at a Michael Jackson or Madonna concert, then the enemy can and does use the same antics in the church so that we will *think* we are seeing the power of God when in fact the spirit of leprosy is in full force. Because it is often times not the true power of God we experience, then we rise up off the floor and come out of our euphoric state with absolutely no change in our hearts. And this is the ultimate goal of the enemy - for us to remain sinful and unchanged while still falling out and speaking in tongues right in the church. The devil is very smart and has studied us to know exactly how to deceive us right in the midst of our own church services. We as preachers must take heed not to be deceived ourselves and not to be used to deceive the people. We must further examine ourselves (Psalm 26:2, 2 Corinthians 13:5) to ensure that we are not spotted with leprosy.

This laying on of hands and "falling out" craze is only a part of all the church sensationalism and ministry antics we entertain. It has gotten to the point that many have grown tired of the church as it is today. There are many who are hungry for God in a real way and are weary of church hype that leaves me with no victory in my soul when all the fanfare is over. We have left Egypt (symbolic of the world) to cross over into Canaan but still find all the characteristics of Egypt in our new dwelling place. We see many claim to be new creatures in Christ according to 2 Corinthians 5:17 and yet remain the same as before God saved many of us. We want to keep the old ways of Egypt while enjoying the fringe benefits of Canaan. Basically, we want one foot in

Canaan and the other foot in Egypt. If we could have it our way, we would reside in Canaan and keep a vacation resort among the Egyptians. Few really want to be sold out to God and forsake the ways of the world and of sin, so we have brought the world and sin with us into our churches. However, it is reported that leprosy started in Egypt where the Bible records Pharoah as being the first to be inflicted with leprosy. It was the Lord's judgment upon him for his sin in not letting the people of Israel go. When God delivered the Israelites from Egypt, they wanted to live in the promised land but also wanted to bring with them the idolatrous, ungodly customs and sins of the Egyptians.

Consequently, God told Israel in Deuteronomy 28:58 - 62 that He would bring upon them the plagues that He inflicted on Egypt if they followed after their unclean practices (idolatry, witchcraft, greed, lies, homosexuality, etc.). And to the church of today, God is saying that since we have brought the ways of spiritual Egypt (the world) into the church, then He has allowed the spirit of leprosy to follow us into our Canaan and it is affecting our promised inheritance. Since we want to play politics and be politically correct in our churches to go along with sin just to get along; since we support lies from the pulpit and competition in our auxiliaries; since we embrace racism and denominational segregation; since we see blind when it comes to homosexuality and bisexuality in our churches and ministries; since we want there to be no difference between gospel music and sensual, enticing carnal music from Egypt, then God said that He will give us what we want and allow leprosy to follow us. This is expressly why our churches are larger and more financially prosperous than they have ever been, yet weaker, more sinful and further from God than they have ever been. We are trying to live in Canaan (mega churches, massive conferences, busy ministries, television programs, etc.) while embracing Egypt (idolatry, lies, homosexuality, greed, position-hungry, etc.) at the same time. The two can not intermingle which is why God commanded Israel not to intermarry with the ungodly because their seed would be contaminated. (Ezra 9:14) Whenever the flesh is allowed to take root among us in the Body of Christ, then whatever is birthed and produced will breed unrighteousness. It is impossible to sow to the flesh and reap righteousness. (Galatians 6:8). We have been blind-sighted by unrighteousness in the church and many want to know how we can get out of the mess that has gripped us. As you continue to partake of this Word of the Lord to you, then you will continue to encounter a cleansing and mounting in the Spirit like never before.

Chapter 2

An Old Leprosy

*W*henever the Bible speaks of hair that is white, it is symbolic of something old (ancient) or something wise. In Daniel 7:9, the prophet says,

> I beheld till the thrones were cast down, and the
> Ancient of days did sit, whose garment was white
> as snow, and the hair of his head like the pure
> wool...

God through Daniel prophesies of Jesus, revealing Him as being the Ancient of days. The word ancient means to be very old; to have qualities associated with age, wisdom or long use; to be old-fashioned or antiquated. Therefore, God the Son is the Everlasting One. He is the oldest being that has ever lived. He is the One whom John speaks of in Revelation 1:8 as being the One "which is, and which was, and which is to come." He has been here forever, knows everything, and has all power.

John further goes on to describe what he saw in a vision that represented Jesus, the Son of man, in Revelation 1:14 where he says,

> His head and his hairs were white like wool, as white as snow...

So, tying in Daniel 7:9 with Revelation 1:14, we see clearly that white hair represents either something old in age or someone wise. Specifically, regarding the case of leprosy, this is why God said that if the leprosy has turned the hair white, then it is an old, ancient leprosy that has been there for a long time. Many churches are extremely set in their old ways. They are stuck in deep-seated traditions that strangle the anointing and put a "DO NOT ENTER" sign up against the Holy Spirit when He wants to come in and take us to a place we have never been before in the Spirit. We do not want to move like Israel with the glory cloud by day and the pillar of fire by night (Exodus 13:21). Not only was the glory cloud and the fire to point the direction for the children of Israel while in the wilderness, but they were for their protection against the elements of this world. The glory cloud during the day was also to cover them from the scorching heat of the natural sun so they would not faint on their journey. Sometimes during our walk with God, if the Lord does not cover us while dealing with the natural elements of this world and the basic issues of life (financial problems, marital issues, tough working conditions, chronic illness, etc.), then we would become overwhelmed, fall by the wayside, and faint. God also used the pillar of fire to keep Israel warm at night from the cold wilderness. This was also their camp fire that kept away bugs, flies, and other pesky insects which are symbolic of evil sprits (Exodus 8:16 - 32). God has designed a plan to keep you guarded against the enemy when for instance he sends people with wrong intentions to destroy you or ungodly prospects that seem like a good opportunity but are sent to sting you. Thank God for the fire of God's glory that burns up every evil work and repels the enemy off of our lives.

Coming from under the glory of God makes you susceptible and vulnerable to the attacks of the enemy. This is expressly why we *need* the glory in our personal lives, homes, ministries and churches. Unfortunately, tradition has choked out the glory that we so desperately need for spiritual health and survival. The enemy knows this, so he keeps a toe-hold in our churches to keep God and His glory out and the traditions of men in. Granted, the apostle Paul says in 2 Thessalonians 2:15:

> Therefore, brethren, stand fast, and hold the traditions which ye have been taught, whether by word, or our epistle.

Paul is referring to holding on to those traditions that are Word-based and orchestrated by the Holy Spirit - not because your grand momma always did it this way or because the deacon's board refuses to budge and go along with the new vision of the pastor. In fact, Jesus rebukes the religious, self-righteous scribes and Pharisees in Matthew 15:3b and verses 6 - 9 where He says:

> ...Why do ye also transgress the commandment of God by your tradition?...Thus, ye have made the commandment of God of none effect by your tradition. Ye hypocrites, well did Esaias prophesy of you saying, "This people draweth nigh unto me with their mouth, and honoureth me with their lips; but their heart is far from me. But in vain they do worship me, teaching for doctrines the

commandments of men."

Jesus says that old, man-made traditions and religion that have no grounding in the Word render God's Word useless and powerless in our lives and is why we remain yoked up and undelivered. Sadly this is the case with many of our churches wherein people are shackled, bound and gagged by these chains. The most deceiving trick to this symptom of leprosy is that the condition has in fact been there such a long time that people have grown accustomed to it, thinking that this is the way things are supposed to be.

This is not talked about or addressed much today, but denominationalism, prejudice and racism are old, traditional issues across the Body of Christ kept alive by the spirit of leprosy. Sunday morning is reported to be the most segregated time not only in our country but throughout the world. What a travesty! Although this is the 21st century, there are still racist bishops, pastors, deacons, choir members, evangelists, ushers, youth leaders, missionaries, etc. who hate their brothers and sisters in Christ from certain ethnic backgrounds. This is still a deep-rooted issue that plagues and separates us, and we think that God is not regarding this wickedness. It is a strong, long-standing weapon of the enemy to keep us divided because there is strength in unity. You can not be of African descent (African American, native African, West Indian, etc.) and hate your Caucasian (Jewish, Irish, Italian, etc.) brothers and sisters. Likewise, you can not truly love God and be a Caucasian, Asian, Egyptian or of any other ethnic group and hate those of African descent and still be in right standing with God. John makes a strong statement where he affirms that "Whosoever hateth his brother is a murderer: and ye know that no murderer hath eternal life abiding in him." (1 John 3:15) This is indeed an old leprosy.

Case in point: My adjutant Karen Michelle Christie and

I were traveling by car to a wedding reception and got lost on the way because the directions were wrong. We ended up in a very remote area with not many buildings or houses around and it was night time. Fortunately, I noticed a little further down the road a beautiful, large church that was having service and had lots of cars on the parking lot. I said to Michelle (the name she goes by), "Oh, look! There's a church down the road. Let's stop there and get directions. I'm sure they'll help us." We then drove to the church, and since Michelle had been driving, I decided I would go inside the church to see if anyone knew how to get to the reception hall we were looking for. While walking through the beautiful church lobby, I could hear music and singing. "How wonderful!," I thought. "It seems like this church is having a great time worshipping God tonight. I wish I could stay and enjoy the service." However, when I walked through the doors of the sanctuary, the vibrant music slowed to a drag, the song leader almost completely stopped singing, and it seemed like the whole congregation turned to look at me with a cold, unwelcoming stare. The entire service basically froze. "Dear Lord!," I thought. You would have thought I was the mafia that just walked in. I knew immediately that I was not welcome there at all - despite all their singing and making melody to the Lord. I was headed to a wedding reception and was dressed nicely, so my attire could not have been the problem. There was simply a problem with my kind coming into their church, and they made it clear under no uncertain terms. Thankfully, they gladly helped me with directions when they found out I had not come to stay for their service.

It is unnerving to know that racism is still much alive in Christendom, even in the midst of our large congregations and great ministries. Even many in our multi-cultural mega churches strongly resent having to worship with others not like themselves and this breeds contention, strife, bitterness, and hatred - all derivatives of the spirit of leprosy. The Apostle Paul says in Colossians 3:11 - 15,

> Where there is neither Greek nor Jew, circumcision nor uncircumcision, Barbarian, Scythian, bond or free: but Christ is all, and in all. Put on therefore, as the elect of God, holy and beloved, bowels of mercies, and kindness, humbleness of mind, meekness, longsuffering; forbearing one another, and forgiving one another, if any man have a quarrel against any: even as Christ forgave you, so also do ye. And above all these things, put on charity [love], which is the bond of perfectness [maturity]. And let the peace of God rule in your hearts, to the which also ye are called in one body and be ye thankful.

Paul is saying that no matter what your ethnic background, Christ is the center and He is in all believers, which makes us one in Him. Not one of us is better than or above the other, and we must be spiritually mature enough to demonstrate love for one another by putting away old past issues that have divided us. Paul goes on to say something really powerful in I Corinthians 13:1 - 3,

> Though I speak with the tongues of men and of angels, and have not charity [love], I am become as sounding brass, or a tinkling cymbal. And though I have the gift of prophecy, and understand all mysteries, and all knowledge; and though I have all faith, so that I could remove mountains, and have not charity [love], I am nothing. And though I bestow all my goods to feed the poor, and though I give my body to be burned, and have not charity [love], it profiteth me nothing.

This is a most revealing and powerful text! You mean to tell me that even though I prophesy, give large offerings to the church, pastor, evangelize, lay hands on the sick, feed the poor, have faith that moves mountains, if I do not have love in my heart the way God commands, then I AM NOTHING?! Absolutely! This is what the Word says, and we can not skip over so-called small matters like racism, bigotry, hatred, prejudice and denominationalism and think that all else that we do is accepted by God. The scripture says it profits you NOTHING! We miss these "little scriptures" that hold back the true blessings of God in our lives. Remember, though, it is the little foxes that spoil the vine (Song of Solomon 2:15) and damage the fruit - and damaged fruit is good for nothing. The church must break free from hatred and racism and must examine itself and deal with this old leprosy that plagues the Body of Christ at large.

Not only has racism, prejudice, and denominationalism inflicted the church for centuries, causing us to remain stuck in old, antiquated division, but there are other strong holds of tradition that keep us in a head lock. It is often the tradition that many belong to churches that their grand momma and great, great grand momma attended but one that has clearly been off course with God for decades and has not helped you spiritually since you were born. The pastor is cheating on his wife, and the church not only knows about it, but either overlooks or accepts it as normal because he has been doing it so long. It is an old leprosy. Sunday sermons have been dry and powerless for years. Nobody has really gotten saved in decades; people only shake the preachers hand and add their names to the church roll. It is an old leprosy. You feel like you are dying of spiritual thirst and starvation and are in dire need of the fresh, life-changing water and manna of the Word of God, but are afraid to leave this kind of church because your whole family is there and that is the family's traditional, dead church. You are also afraid your family and the church will turn against you for seeking a fresh Word from God elsewhere. [There are many cases like this across the Body of Christ.] You have been warned that if you leave this church, then the family will get angry with you and may even stop dealing with you. That may be the reason your family is stuck, bound and can not get a breakthrough because the name Ichabod may be written on the doorpost of your church (1 Samuel 4:21). Ichabod means that the glory of the Lord has departed from a place. You can easily diagnose this symptom because there is no anointing, no deliverance, no salvation, no glory, no fire, or no edification - just plain old leprosy. You struggle Sunday after Sunday to tolerate being in an environment where the people seem like the walking dead - spiritually lifeless. Only a select few people seem to even think there is anything wrong with the church because others have gotten stuck in this old, traditional rut claiming that "it's been this way for years." This is another chief symptom of the spirit of leprosy. It turns the hair white until eventually the hair thins and falls out. Hair represents the glory of God. Is the glory seeping out of your ministry or has it completely departed?

The spirit of intimidation abounds in this kind of leprous church that practices ungodly traditions because the devil certainly does not want to give up ground he has controlled for years. For years it has been the case in some churches that the deacons or trustees control the pastor. If the pastor does not preach a message to their liking or touches on their area of sin, then he is threatened to be shut down and kicked out. Flesh has always wanted to dominate and control the church and limit the hand of God. This is why any effort to change tradition in this kind of infirmed, traditional church will be challenged like a junkyard dog.

However, since when has the Bible instructed that the priest follow the instructions of the people? God gave the priests specific orders on how to minister in His temple, and as long as the priest stayed right with God, then He would always be directed by the voice of God and had answers for the people of God. In fact, when Aaron (the high priest) and Miriam (the prophetess) who were leaders in Israel and siblings of Moses tried to come against him because of their own fleshly jealousy, the Lord reprimanded them both, explaining to them his anger over them opposing Moses in Numbers 12:6 - 8 where He says,

> ...Listen to My words: When a prophet of the Lord is among you, I reveal myself to him in visions, I speak to him in dreams. But this is not true of My servant Moses; he is faithful in all My house. With him I speak face to face, clearly and not in riddles; he sees the form of the Lord. Why then were you not afraid to speak against My servant Moses? (LASB)

In other words, the Lord was telling Aaron and Miriam who were leaders second in command to Moses that He speaks face to face with Moses and therefore Moses as the "chief shepherd" of Israel had already heard from Him on how to lead the nation. So, what caused Aaron and Miriam to think they had the right to oppose a man whom the hand of God rested heavily upon and who was directly connected with the Master of the universe - the one with all wisdom, knowledge, and power? It was their own selfish, carnal motives in operation. They were envious of Moses' power and influence. Since they could not find fault with the way he led the children of Israel, they chose to criticize him marrying a Cushite woman. Trying to hinder the man or woman of God who is charged with a divine assignment (whoever they may be) is like trying to diametrically oppose the work of the Lord since He is the one that called them in order to complete a work. Can you imagine the weight on Moses' shoulders to lead over one million people out of Egypt, through the wilderness and into Canaan? God was using Moses for an arduous task which is why He would not allow anyone (not church leadership or family) to become a thorn to impede progress on the journey to Canaan. That is the reason God clearly commands in 1 Chronicles 16:22, "...Touch not mine anointed, and do my prophets no harm." God was so serious about Moses that He not only spoke up for him, but He struck Miriam with leprosy as punishment for coming against the plan of God through Moses. It is a dangerous thing for church leadership for self-motivated fleshy reasons to try to yoke up and bind the hands of a pastor who is anointed by and unified with the Almighty.

God through His Holy Spirit runs His own church and uses a pastor to spearhead His work. The deacons, trustees, ministers, missionaries, mother's board, women's ministry, choir, usher board, etc. are all there to help carry out the work given to the pastor. Some of our churches are so leprous that the pastor is held hostage by the "traditional church mafia" who threatens to vote him out or yank his salary if he does not abide by their old, ancient demands. No one dares to speak up because it has been this way for years, and addressing this issue deems you a devil. But I hear the Lord saying that as you read this book, the spirit of the Lord is charging your heart to pull down these traditional strongholds and to war in the Spirit in fasting and praying for true deliverance from the traditional spirit of leprosy that has strongly affected your church. The Spirit of the Lord is more than able and through your prayers will destroy this yoke of bondage over your family, pastor, auxiliaries, and church at large. If Esther's fasting and praying could save a nation, surely yours can save your home and your church. Declare to yourself that deliverance is on the way!

Chapter 3

Struck In The Forehead

Truth Symptom #3:
*~ Leprosy could get in your forehead, cut you
off from the house of God, and cause you to
dwell in a separate house ~*

"And Uzziah the king was a leper…and dwelt in a
several house, being a leper; for he was cut off
from the house of the Lord."
2 Chronicles 26:21

*K*ing Uzziah (2 Chronicles 26) was a great king, following after the godly example of his father King
Amaziah. He sought earnestly after God by seeking the
advice and counsel of the prophet Zechariah. His humility
and obedience to the Lord caused him to prosper in war
against many enemies and in enormous wealth and riches.
He strategically reconstructed broken down cities. King
Uzziah became very well known and respected around the
world for his military strength, great wealth, and his ability
to build cities.

However, 2 Chronicles 26:16 - 21 recounts the following:

But when he [Uzziah] was strong, his heart was
lifted up to his destruction: for he transgressed

against the Lord his God, and went into the temple of the Lord to burn incense upon the altar of incense. And Azariah the priest went in after him, and with him fourscore priests of the Lord, that were valiant men: and they withstood Uzziah the king, and said unto him, "It appertaineth not unto thee, Uzziah, to burn incense unto the Lord, but to the priests the sons of Aaron, that are consecrated to burn incense: go out of the sanctuary; for thou hast trespassed; neither shall it be for thine honour from the Lord God. Then Uzziah was wroth, and had a censer in his hand to burn incense: and while he was wroth with the priests, the leprosy even rose up in his forehead before the priests in the house of the Lord, from beside the incense altar. And Azariah the chief priest, and all the priests, looked upon him, and, behold, he was leprous in his forehead, and they thrust him out from thence; yea, himself hasted also to go out, because the Lord had smitten him. And Uzziah the king was a leper unto the day of his death, and dwelt in a several house, being a leper; for he was cut off from the house of the Lord..."

The most tragic thing about Uzziah's case is that he started out righteous and ended up leprous. Although God prospered him in material possessions, military might and a great name, once Uzziah reached the pinnacle of his success, he became "strong" in his own might and abandoned the law of the Lord. He became so strong that he began a destructive journey down a path right out of the will of God and ended up trying to serve in an area of ministry that was completely "out of bounds" for the office he walked in. Uzziah was a king and not a priest. Only the priests were ordained and consecrated by God to burn incense before the

Lord. Therefore, Uzziah was operating illegally in the kingdom; but because he was the king, he thought that he was
above the law and that the Word of God did not apply to
him. His *heart was lifted up* in dangerous, self-willed pride.
Pride is the precursor to rebellion which the Bible says is as
the sin of witchcraft. (1 Samuel 15:23) Further, Proverbs
16:18 declares that "Pride goeth before destruction, and a
haughty spirit before a fall." First Timothy 3:6 speaks of the
peril of "being lifted up with pride," while Jeremiah 49:16
talks about the "the pride of thine heart." So, essentially,
Uzziah got to the point where it was all about him. And even
though 80 priests approached him about his sin to challenge
and correct him to stop his madness, Uzziah refused to
repent, got mad and continued on operating in an area of
ministry that God forbid him to. How precarious!

Unfortunately, the church is laced with many spiritual
Uzziahs who started out in right alignment with God, but
have since been derailed by their own selfish desires birthed
out of rebellion and pride. You remember when you first got
saved, had just started your own ministry or had just
launched out into the deep based on a vision God gave you?
Your intent was to depend solely on the Lord Jesus for direction - out of fear of failure if nothing else. But as soon as
things began to flourish and spiritual success began to kick
in, then you felt like Uzziah that you no longer needed God
and turned a deaf ear to the voice of the Lord, deceived by
the adversary to think that you could make it without divine
instruction. [Have we forgotten that Jesus said, "...without
Me ye can do nothing?" (John 15:5b)] This is a classic pit-
fall for many pastors whom the Lord leads to start a church.
In the beginning of the ministry when it is small and does
not have many members or much money, the pastor's heart
is very tender and sensitive toward God. He does not want
to miss the will of God at all. He recognizes that the very
existence of his new church rests in the Master's hand and

on the divine leading of the Almighty. There are all night prayer meetings, the pastor shows true concern for the members, the man or woman of God is constantly seeking out of the mouth of the prophet a rhema Word from the Lord, the prophetic is warmly received for rebuke or for encouragement, etc. However, as soon as the membership starts growing to significant numbers, the money starts rolling in, the pastor's name begins to become known for the so-called great work he is doing with the ministry, then a strong spirit of delusion hits many of our leaders. Prayer meetings cease; and they often begin to abuse the sheep, misappropriate funds and claim the glory that belongs to God. We try to pimp God for our own selfish motives so that He will raise us up to great ministry or so that we can get the house, car or husband we want. Many worship Him out of false pretenses only because we want Him to do something for us, but rarely because we sincerely love Him. The spirit of leprosy has us so desperate for things and carnal possessions that we have totally missed the mark.

Matthew Henry's Commentary documents that leprosy was considered a disease that would bury you alive. You were considered to be the walking dead because even though you were physically still alive, you were so infirmed, sick and spotted that you were cut off from God, the temple, the people and society until you actually did physically die. He also was required to cry from afar off, "Unclean! Unclean!" This is so parallel to many of our ministries and spiritual lives today. A leprous ministry may function week after week doing all the things that seem to show signs of life, when in fact all these mechanics amount to nothing but a lot of dead works of the flesh because the life of the Spirit is not in what we do. Do you wonder why certain people with foul spirits are avoided "like the plague" as we commonly say today? It is because they harbor the spirit of leprosy which reaks from them, crying, "Unclean! Unclean!" Their spirits are warning you saying,

"Life unclean!" "Heart unclean!" "Ways unclean!" "Intentions unclean!" Churches and ministries fall in the same leprous predicament when people begin to drop off and congregations dwindle because of prevailing sin, filth and idolatry; and others may not know the inside dirt, but all they will sense coming from the ministry is this: "Unclean! Unclean!"

If you are a pastor or ministry leader, you may be at a place where you are finding that your church is on a downward slope. You recognize that the Spirit of God does not move in your midst so you try your best to "work it." People are no longer really drawn to your services and for some reason many are leaving your church. To "spice up the church" and increase attendance, you have tried to consider what kinds of programs and other ideas you could come up with to make a difference, but nothing so far has worked. You are frustrated and are desperate for an answer. However, the answer is not in the programs, it is not in increased attendance, or in copying what you see the other church doing around the corner. The answer is in the life of the Spirit, in getting on your face before God and crying out to God asking Him to purge your own heart from dead works. Hebrews 9:14 says,

> How much more shall the blood of Christ, who through the eternal Spirit offered Himself without spot to God, purge your conscience from dead works to serve the living God?

You must seek after God with your whole heart and ask the Lord to show you what it is *in you* that God wants to cleanse and purge. Often times it is not our churches that are on a downward slope, it is us and our relationship and walk with God that are declining. As a result, we begin to do like Uzziah and go off on our own plan, ideas and agenda. We begin to operate "out of bounds" doing things that God never ordained us to do. This pushes us further and further away from His will because now our destructive will has taken over. And the manifestation of all this shows up in our churches and our ministries because we are the heads of these works.

God struck King Uzziah (the leader) with leprosy right in the place symbolic of the root of his disobedience - his forehead which represents the will or the mind. Since Uzziah's will was in direct opposition to the will of the Lord, despite being forewarned by 80 valiant men of God to discontinue operating according to his own fleshly will, God gave him exactly what he wanted and tattooed his mind with the flesh to the point of his own destruction. When you refuse to repent and turn from what you know displeases God, He will allow you to have it your way which will lead you to your own demise. When your forehead is leprous, every thing you think, plan, or desire is originated out of quick raw flesh. You preach, prophesy and sing for your own glory and not the glory of God. You politic for position and will try to destroy anybody that gets in the way of the position you lust after. You "prophelie" because you want to impress others, but you really do not have a Word from the Lord. You flatter for an opportunity to minister on major platforms. You sell out holiness to fit in with the unrighteous clique in the church. You do not preach a convicting gospel for fear of the response of the people. You want to save your reputation instead of making yourself of no reputation like Jesus (Philippians 2:7). You are seriously leprous in your forehead, the seat of your mind and your will. Everything you do will be birthed out of sin and flesh and will not pros-per at all. Do not let the size of your church or ministry fool you to believe that all is well because there are many large, leprous churches and ministries across the globe. The inter-esting thing about God is that He will sometimes give you what you asked for to prove that what you thought you wanted was not what you needed. Often what we ask of God is so low grade that we forfeit the real blessings that He has reserved for us as we walk in righteousness. We seek after houses and cars and God wants to give us power. We seek after large ministries and God wants to give us a demon-chasing anointing. We seek after positions, when God says that there is a place (a position) by Him that will provoke the glory. (Exodus 33:21) These are the dead works that have clinched the church.

God wants to deliver you from the dead works that have separated you from His presence, where He dwells. These dead works of the flesh have spotted you and your ministry with the spirit of leprosy that has cut you off from the true tabernacle of the Lord, causing you to dwell in a "several" or severed house separated from the remnant - the true people of God. This is why some say, "It don't take all that" when it comes to praise, worship, righteous living, holiness and purification. It is because they live spiritually in a separate house, cut off from God's true dwelling place. Jesus said in John 14:2 - 3,

> In my Father's house are many mansions: if it were not so, I would have told you. I go to prepare a place for you. And if I go and prepare a place for you, I will come again, and receive you unto Myself; that where I am, there ye may be also."

When Jesus spoke this, He was not on His way to heaven as many have thought, but He was on His way to the cross. We are so materialistic in our thinking that we thought Jesus was speaking of preparing us a mansion in the sky made of brick and mortar like we live in here on earth. On the contrary, there is nothing physical or fleshly in heaven. There will be no cement, plaster, wood or siding there. So, if you want a physical house to live in, you better buy one right here on earth because you will be extremely disappointed in heaven when you recognize that Jesus did `not mean that He was going to build you a house with a kitchen, two bathrooms, a den, a fireplace and a Jacuzzi. The word *mansions* translates to mean *dwelling places*. So, because of the blood of Jesus that was shed for our sins on the cross, we now have access to a new dwelling place in Him. You can either dwell in the Outer Court, Inner Court or the Holy of Holies. However, God never designed for you to dwell in the Outer Court which is the place of the flesh; but He intended and prepared for you to come and dwell or live with Him in the third dimension which is the place of the Spirit. That is why Jesus said, "that where I am, there ye may be also." The Spirit of our great God and Savior Jesus Christ dwells in the Holy of Holies. If you lived spiritually in the true tabernacle of the Holy Spirit not made by physical, fleshly hands (Hebrews 8:2), then your soul would embrace holiness which is the very nature and essence of God. This is why God commands us in Leviticus 11:44 "...be holy; for I am holy." Remember that without holiness, no man in his spotted flesh will even be able to discern, understand or recognize God. (Hebrews 12:14)

Chapter 4

Leprous From Head To Foot

> ***Truth Symptom #4:***
> *~ Leprosy can spread across the entire body*
> *from head to toe - everywhere you look ~*
>
> "And if leprosy break out abroad in the skin, and
> the leprosy cover all the skin of him that hath
> the plague from his head even to his foot,
> wheresoever the priest looketh..."
> Leviticus 13:12

*G*od said that another indicator of the effects of leprosy
was that it could break out and cover the body from
head to toe - every where the priest looked. Can you imagine the grossness of fleshly, weeping sores or blemishes
spread over a person's entire body, including their head?
How grotesque and sad. Like the leprous man gravely
affected across his entire body by this plague, there has likewise been a break out of fleshly sin in the church from head
to toe - from the pulpit to the pew member. It does not matter how long you have been saved, what your position or title
is, what church you belong to, how long you have been pastoring, what denomination you belong to, etc., this debilitating spirit has no respect of persons or members when it
comes to affecting the Body.

Paul speaks in 1 Corinthians 12:12 - 26 of how the church

or Body of Christ is likened to the members or parts of a natural body. Just to highlight a portion of this text to make a point, specifically in 1 Corinthians 12:12, 14 - 18 he says:

> For as the body is one, and hath many members, and all the members of that one body, being many, are one body: so also is Christ...For the body is not one member, but many. If the foot shall say, "because I am not the hand, I am not of the body"; is it therefore not of the body? And if the ear shall say, "because I am not the eye, I am not of the body"; is it therefore not of the body? If the whole body were an eye, where were the hearing? If the whole were hearing, where were the smelling? But now hath God set the members every one of them in the body, as it hath pleased him.

Here Paul is saying that the church Body of believers is similar to a physical body that has many members but all the members make up one body. He uses for examples the foot which could symbolize one with an evangelistic anointing to travel from place to place preaching the gospel; the hand which could represent one with the gift of healing; the ear which could be symbolic of a member with a prophetic gift; and the eye which could refer to one with spiritual discernment. So, when leprosy would break out across the entire body from head to toe, it had no limitations or exemptions when it came to what part of the body it would hit.

Consequently, the spirit of leprosy in the church has broken out every where you look. All across the Body, there is leprous flesh on parade. It is in the feet. There is an epidemic among our evangelists, several of whom are crooked and competitive. Evangelistic preaching has become a career and is rarely approached like a true calling. My career focuses on money, wealth, and promotion while my calling focuses on salvation, deliverance, and the divine will of God. Many preach only to make money instead of for the edification of the Body of Christ (Ephesians 4:12) and for the salvation of the lost. We are anxious to see how many engagements we can garner like trophies on a mantle because this pumps up our flesh. We compare ourselves to our peers to see who has preached at the largest churches and who has the best "hoop and holler." However, there is much more to preaching than just style and technique or a hoop and a holler. Anybody can holler and make noise, but not everybody can rebuke demons, destroy yokes and deliver divine revelation that changes lives. I have heard on countless occasions preachers who would scream over the pulpit literally saying nothing of substance at all. But because his or her screaming and yelling in the microphone had a nice sound or hum to it that appealed to the flesh, then the people would go crazy in support of these shenanigans. This always encouraged the empty preacher who is no more than sounding brass and tinkling symbol to continue his or her leprous ways and to deliver no meat of the Word to God's flock.

Preaching has become desirable and glamorous because of the Hollywood-style image that the church has adopted. We treat our preachers like movie stars, requesting autographs and chasing after them like the paparazzi. Every where you look, somebody's main desire, focus, or intent is to become a celebrity preacher with all the glitz and glamour of Hollywood packaged in church form. For this reason, thousands and thousands of those in the feet of the leprous Body anxiously run to label themselves as evangelists when God never called them - their leprous flesh called them. One of the key questions we need to ask ourselves as evangelists is this: Outside of God, who in the church called you into the preaching ministry and affirmed publicly what God said about you behind closed doors? Who was there? Where are your witnesses? You should be able to point to the day that God affirmed your calling officially before men - the day he used a man or woman of God to validate your ministry. You can identify in scripture the place where God called Moses, Saul, David, the twelve disciples, and many, many more. Even God the Father affirmed the ministry of Jesus and announced Him on the Mount of Transfiguration when He said in Mark 9:7, "This is My beloved Son: hear him." Once the flesh of Jesus began to dissipate and the glory of God was visibly manifest in Him, God spoke from heaven and called attention to every ear to hear His voice. Likewise, when transformation takes place in you to the point where the activity of your flesh decreases to nothing and the glory of God is visibly manifest on your life, then God will speak from the throne room and command attention to your evangelistic and/or prophetic voice.

If you are an evangelist who views the preaching ministry as a ticket to stardom, then let me inform you of the truth of the matter because somewhere along the way, you have gotten a hold of advice about the ministry that was contaminated with leprosy. Preaching the unadulterated gospel is a death walk for a sold-out evangelist. Your message will cause your crucifixion, and there is nothing glamorous about being on death row when it comes to killing your flesh. You must die daily to your own "hoop and holler" and let God give you a voice that will blow the true trumpet in Zion. (Joel 2:1) There will be challenging times when your spirit will wrestle with the will of God and you will not want to preach what you hear God saying to the church because this leprous generation is accustomed to candy and not nourishing meat. Leprosy in the feet has caused malnourishment in the Body. However, when you crucify your own flesh and take up your cross to really follow Jesus and become a present-day disciple of Christ, the power of the Spirit will heighten in you to a degree that will astonish you. Righteousness will open doors for you in ministry that no man can shut (Revelation 3:8). The Master is waiting for His Bride (the church) to de-robe flesh and put on the wedding garments of righteousness.

Speaking of wedding garments, the Bible likens the relationship between Adam and Eve to that of Christ and His Bride (the church). Just as Adam was the head of Eve, Christ is also the head of the church according to Ephesians 5:23. The term *head* in this case means governor, covering or supreme leader. Therefore, although Eve had her own physical head on her body, Adam was not considered to be that kind of head; but he was her covering, the governor and supreme leader of the marital relationship and family unit. Likewise, the church or Bride of Christ has its own spiritual head which represents the leadership (pastors, bishops, apostles, elders, etc.) of the church, but Christ is the Covering, Governor and Supreme Leader. There is absolutely nothing wrong with the Supreme Head of the church which is Christ; however, leprosy has hard struck the headship or leadership (representing the head) of the church which is overall in dire need of transformation and cleansing.

Many of our leaders have gotten off track with God and have decided to operate according to their own will instead of the will of God - just like King Uzziah. Because many pastors have gone out and started churches on their own accord without being called of God, we have a massive number of unhealthy ministries birthed out of self-will, competition and church splits. There is no longer real accountability when it comes to how many of our pastors today handle the Lord's business and His sheep. The pastor can claim that God spoke a thing, when he has not heard from God at all. The majority of pastors today are without accountability to a senior leader or bishop. The early church was governed by the council of apostles and elders in Jerusalem to shake out issues and maintain order in the Lord's church. (Acts 8:14, 16:4) This being the case, then the question becomes this: Who is there to keep you on track and ensure the integrity of the gospel you preach or the things you do? Who is there to ensure that you do not abuse the sheep and mishandle the church affairs? Proverbs 11:14 says that "Where no counsel is, the people fall; but in the multitude of counsellors there is safety." A one-man ship being run by one with no godly counsel is a tragic accident waiting to happen.

This epidemic is bad in the church because fleshly desires cause so many to seek to become overnight wonders who just pop up out of obscurity with no affirmation from a spiritual leader (i.e. spiritual father or mother). My father (Suffragan Bishop Lawrence E. Brown, Sr.) would always say regarding today's pastors and preachers, "Some were called, some were sent and some just packed their bags and went." No one called many of the so-called pastors in the church today; they just stepped out on their own fleshly will and went. Often times when a leader in the church becomes angry with the pastor and does not agree with the direction that the man or woman of God is taking or because the pastor does not allow this leader to do what he or she wants, then the leader under that pastor is soon to break rank, run off and start their own ministry. This is why every time you turn around some other "Minister Joe Blow" or "Prophetess Jane Doe" is starting another church which is established by an inexperienced hireling looking for a chance to do his or her own thing and shine like the noon day sun. But my question for many of the pastors today is this: Who sent you out as a shepherd? You may say that you do not need man's affirmation, but according to scripture, every king that God appointed and those sent out in New Testament leadership were anointed for their office *by a man*. Saul was anointed by Samuel (1 Samuel 10:1). David was anointed by the men of Judah (2 Samuel 2:4). Paul (Saul) and Barnabas were anointed through the Holy Spirit by the leaders of the church at Antioch (Acts 13:1 - 4). Then Paul turns around and disciples and affirms the young pastor Timothy (1 & 2 Timothy). Jesus (God manifested as *a man*) called and sent out the twelve disciples or apostles who were the first apostles and leaders in the Lord's church (Mark 3:14 - 19, 6:7 - 11). Given this pattern in scripture, how is it that we think that the order of God has changed and that we need no one to appoint us to the office of the pastorate or send us forth as ministers? None of us is authorized to void out the Word and pattern of God, making it ineffective in our lives. (Matthew 15:6) We have gotten far away from the instructions that God has left the church for the sake of order and accountability. And we wonder why our churches are unhealthy. Could it be because you as a pastor or leader are out of order? Could it be leprosy in the headship of our churches?

In Numbers 33:54, the Lord tells Moses,

> And ye shall divide the land by lot for an inheritance among your families: and to the more ye shall give the more inheritance, and to the fewer ye shall give the less inheritance: every man's inheritance shall be in the place where his lot falleth; *according to the tribes of your fathers ye shall inherit*.

What is God saying here? The Lord is establishing the fact that your inheritance is directly linked to your father's portion. Therefore it is important to be in alignment with your spiritual father in order to release the blessings coming from the many years of his labor in God. The enemy understands the power of this divine principle; and this is the supreme reason why the adversary has caused countless men and women of God to come from under their spiritual father and his covering. Satan's desire is to cut off your inheritance that comes according to what your father received from God. What a powerful divine illumination!

Another chief problem that needs mentioning briefly

when it comes to leprosy in the head is that we live in a time like the days and function of King Jeroboam. Jehovah God spoke to Jeroboam to warn him about his evil ways, but 1 Kings 13: 33 - 34 says,

> Even after this, Jeroboam did not change his evil ways, but once more appointed priests for the high places from all sorts of people. Anyone who wanted to become a priest he consecrated for the high places. This was the sin of the house of Jeroboam that led to its downfall and to its destruction from the face of the earth. (LASB)

Jeroboam appointed as priests anybody that wanted to be a priest or minister in the Lord's temple and chose these so-called priests from the lowest and most common of the people. In other words, whoever wanted to be a preacher, Jeroboam licensed or ordained a preacher. It did not matter whether or not they were of the lineage of Aaron like God instructed in Exodus 28:1. The Word of God declares that this was an evil thing in the sight of the Lord. The present day church has followed the same ungodly practices of Jeroboam. Many pastors make preachers out of whoever wants to be a preacher. We license and ordain our friends, our families, those who give large tithes and big offerings, people that we do not want to leave our churches, etc. Being a friend of the pastor does not automatically make you a preacher. Just because you are in the pastor's family does not validate you as an evangelist. Neither can you buy your way into the prophetic ministry through your tithes and offerings. They are the Lord's (Leviticus 27:30, Malachi 3:8) and not yours to manipulate the headship of the church. Granted, there are pastors who do in fact have friends, family and others that are truly called alongside them to carry the preached gospel, but I am speaking of the many situations where being made a priest is based on church politics and is intended as a reward from the pastor for some carnal reason rather than God calling you into ministry. This same sin that led to Jeroboam's downfall and destruction is what plagues the Body today. It is imperative that church leadership seriously hear from God concerning the appointment of the preachers that minister to God's people.

However, because leprosy has affected the ears and eyes of the Body, many can not hear the true voice of God and discern His direction. Regarding the ears of the Body of Christ, the book of Revelation and other scriptures constantly repeat, "He that hath an ear, let him hear what the Spirit saith unto the churches." (Revelation 2:7, 11, 17, 29; 3:6, 13, Matthew 11:15, Luke 8:8) This is spoken several times because there is a serious need in this end time to hear the authentic voice of God. Because we are not in a place to really hear God, we end up lying and saying things we never *heard* God say. In Jeremiah 23:29 - 32 God says,

> Is not My Word like as a fire? saith the Lord: and like a hammer that breaketh the rock in pieces? Therefore, behold, I am against the prophets, saith the Lord, that steal My words every one from his neighbour. Behold, I am against the prophets, saith the Lord, that use their tongues, and say, He saith. Behold, I am against them that prophesy false dreams, saith the Lord, and do tell them, and cause My people to err by their lies, and by their lightness; yet I sent them not, nor commanded them: therefore they shall not profit this people at all, saith the Lord.

Jehovah God inquires through the prophet Jeremiah to remind the people that His true Word is like fire that burns up everything that is not holy and purifies the righteous. It

61

burns up the nastiness of the flesh (jealousy, competition, high-mindedness, disorder, selfish motives, evil intentions, false humility, vain glory, self exaltation, homosexuality, adultery, etc.) and purifies us to a higher level of sanctification and righteousness that will result in a powerful prayer life, sincere humility, truth in our mouths, and a life of real consecration to God. These are the effects of the true Word of God that is like a hammer that breaks up the fallow ground in our lives, churches, and ministries. It is impossible to sit under the unadulterated gospel and not be changed from the inside out. Since His Word is like fire and a hammer, something must either burn up, become more purified, or break in us as a result of the power of the authentic, raw Word of God. The problem is that we can not hear God in order to speak His true Word, and therefore, we conjure up false dreams and prophelie because we are hard-pressed to impress the flesh. Yet, our empty preaching and prophelying does not profit or benefit the people at all, just as God said. And for this reason, the people generally remain the same.

As for the eyes of the Body, again, as mentioned earlier, our spiritual discernment at large is weak and off. We really can not see God and discern what is God and what is of the enemy in our churches. Leprosy in our churches has caused us to become spiritually blind, walking like a man stumbling in the dark. We are seeing things with the eyes of the flesh which causes us to desire what God has not ordained for us. For instance, it seems that massive numbers think they *see themselves* as and are becoming bishops these days to the point that it has cheapened the real meaning and sanctity of this office in the eyes of the people. Everybody wants to be a bishop, but not everybody is called to be a bishop. Yes, it looks glamorous to the fleshly eye, but is that what God sees for you? Are spiritual cataracts clouding your vision? The fact that there are pseudo-bishops that God has not ordained

usurping this office does not take away from the true power
and sacredness of the bishopric. We must remember that for
every real thing, there is always a counterfeit to contend. For
every truth that is spoken, there is a lie released from the pit
of hell to compete against it in order to confuse the people.
As people of God, we must become more discerning with
our spiritual eyes to recognize and receive the real and reject
the counterfeit. We must come out of the dark and turn the
light on so that we can see the movement and activity of the
true hand of God. First John 1:5b declares "...that God is
light, and in Him is no darkness at all." David says in Psalm
119:105, "Thy Word is a lamp unto my feet, and a light unto
my path." Then John 1:1, 4, 5, 9 declares,

> In the beginning was the Word, and the Word was
> with God, and the Word was God...In Him was
> life, and the life was the light of men. And the
> Light shineth in darkness; and the darkness com-
> prehended it not...That was the true Light, which
> lighteth every man that cometh into the world."

Jesus further says in John 8:12,

> ...I am the light of the world: he that followeth me
> shall not walk in darkness, but shall have the light
> of life.

With Jesus and His Word being our light, what causes us
not to be able to see spiritually? The answer is that leprosy
has inflicted the inner eyes of the church. But, the good
news for us is that the light of God has the power to shine so
bright that it drives out the darkness overshadowing us as a
result of the spirit of leprosy. Our ears and eyes can be
cleansed from what plagues us so that we can truly hear
what the Spirit is saying to the church and see the move of

God from the third realm. I strongly believe that our time has come to be cleansed in our inner man and break free from the flesh.

Chapter 5

Miriam, A Leper?

Truth Symptom #5:
~ Anybody could be struck with or have leprosy ~

"And the cloud departed from off the tabernacle;
and behold, Miriam became leprous, white as snow:
and Aaron looked upon Miriam, and,
behold, she was leprous."
Numbers 12:10

---

*A*s the Lord led me to search out what His Word declares regarding the spirit of leprosy, it was even convicting for me to look into the mirror of the Word and realize some areas where I had been spotted by the flesh and needed God to cleanse and renew me. No one is above being inflicted to some degree with spiritual leprosy. In fact, Paul warns us in 1 Corinthians 10:12 "Wherefore let him that thinketh he standeth take heed lest he fall." In other words, whenever you think that you are above reproach and that there is nothing at all wrong with your walk with God, then you are blind-sighted and in grave danger. Even if you contend with the so-called little things, the Bible still declares in Song of Solomon 2:15 that it is the little foxes that spoil the vines and destroy the fruit in your life. No matter who you are or what position you hold, until the day you depart this life, you remain a prime candidate and susceptible to the plague of leprosy. As long as we live in these bodies, these earthen vessels, we must contend with the war between our flesh and the Spirit of God. Therefore, anybody could be inflicted with leprosy.

Oddly enough, we have been persuaded to believe that if a person has a large church, a seemingly prosperous evangelistic or healing ministry, a powerful prophetic gift, a thriving religious business, an anointed music ministry, etc., that he or she could not possibly have any serious spiritual issues. People this prosperous in the kingdom do not contend with the spirit of leprosy - just look at how famous they are or how powerful their ministries or how much they have accomplished in their walk with God, right? WRONG! These are the ones who are prime targets for the enemy to inflict and spot with leprous, fleshly blemishes. Why? It is because by being accomplished or successful in ministry, it is proven that these individuals can affect the masses. If the enemy can get them entangled in proud flesh and self-willed motives against the will of God, then he can in turn affect millions through the sin of one well-regarded, influential leper. Do any come to mind off the top of your head?

From the least to the greatest, there is no person too high and mighty or too lowly and insignificant that the enemy does not strongly consider as next members in the spiritual leprous hall of fame. Among the roll call of lepers that the Bible speaks of are the following:

- Miriam, the prophetess
- Naaman, captain of the Syrian army
- Simon, labeled "Simon the leper"
- Uzziah, the king
- Gehazi, servant to Elisha
- Pharoah, ruler of Egypt
- The 10 lepers, who were common folk
- The four lepers at the gate of Samaria

• The man "full of leprosy" healed by Jesus

Although we will not deal with every case of leprosy that the scriptures speak of, we will however highlight a few instances that can help us to understand that this spiritual plague is not limited to unregenerate winos and prostitutes on the streets. But, it is very active at every level along the social stratum, in every denomination, among every ethnic group, within the upper and lower ministerial echelons, etc. Clearly, as you can see from the list above, the plague of leprosy had no respect of persons or position. Absolutely anybody could be inflicted with leprosy. And this is why we at every level of ministry and in our walk with the Lord *must* keep our hearts clean before God.

We talk about Uzziah thoroughly and mention Pharoah in other segments of this book, so we will not rehearse their details here. However, let us reconsider Miriam in more detail and also highlight the case of Gehazi and Naaman.

As mentioned in another chapter, Miriam was struck with leprosy as a result of defying and coming against Moses along with their brother Aaron. She was a most influential spiritual leader who helped Moses govern Israel. She was therefore very well known, and get this…Miriam was also a prophetess. You mean to tell me that you can be a prophetess one moment and the next be a fleshly, spiritual leper? Absolutely! The hand of the Lord was heavily upon Moses for the sake of leading Israel through the wilderness toward the promise land. That was a major task and God was not going to allow jealousy, pride, selfishness, high-mindedness, self-righteousness, or any other ungodly, fleshly stumbling block to hamper the purpose. Miriam tried to hinder the Lord's work and was immediately struck with a judgment. The Bible recounts in Numbers 12:1 - 5; 9, 10, 15,

And Miriam and Aaron spake against Moses because of the Ethiopian woman whom he had married: for he had married an Ethiopian woman. And they said, Hath the Lord indeed spoken only by Moses? hath He not also spoken by us? And the Lord heard it...And the Lord spake suddenly unto Moses, and unto Aaron, and unto Miriam, Come ye out ye three unto the tabernacle of the congregation. And they three came out. And the Lord came down in the pillar of the cloud, and stood in the door of the tabernacle, and called Aaron and Miriam: and they both came forth...And the anger of the Lord was kindled against them; and he departed. And the cloud departed from off the tabernacle; and, behold, Miriam became leprous, white as snow: and Aaron looked upon Miriam, and, behold, she was leprous...And Miriam was shut out from the camp seven days: and the people journeyed not until Miriam was brought in again.

Notice that all three leaders (Moses, Aaron, and Miriam) were present at this particular scene. Then from the pillar of the cloud God called out Aaron and Miriam and rebuked them for opposing Moses. When the glory cloud of His presence lifted, all three were left standing there but Miriam was the only one who had been struck with leprosy. I often wondered why it was that although both Aaron and Miriam came against Moses, only Miriam was inflicted with leprosy and not Aaron. Well, the antiquities of Matthew Henry state that Miriam was apparently the one who instigated and initiated the rise against Moses and was therefore punished. Again as stated before, the real problem Aaron and Miriam had with Moses was not the fact that he had married an Ethiopian woman, but it was because of their jealousy over him being the most powerful man in Israel at the time. They complain in Numbers 12:2 that Moses is not the only one that God speaks through and that the Lord also spoke through them - just like He did Moses. So the bottom line is that they were envious of his position both with the people and with God and sought to bring contention and division in the camp. God was not about to tolerate their mess.

Some historians speculate that Miriam (as a big sister to Moses) was also possibly envious of Moses' Ethiopian wife because with the new wife coming on the scene, Miriam could have felt threatened by another woman who would have potentially greater influence on Moses than she was accustomed to having. Being a woman myself, I can testify that there are few things in the world worse or more destructive than a jealous, malicious woman. Song of Solomon 8:6 says,

> ...jealousy is cruel as the grave: the coals thereof
> are coals of fire, which hath a most vehement fire.

Whether jealous of Moses alone or of his Ethiopian wife as well, Miriam's bitter jealousy and resentment was the root to what gave birth to the plague of leprosy on her life. Have you ever encountered someone (or yourself maybe) who seemed to be on a vehement mission to destroy someone else's reputation or scandalize their name for no apparent reason? You find that this person conjures up lies about the other individual in order to taint people's perception of them. And if asked what is the reason for their severe dislike - almost to the point of hatred - they give unsubstantiated answers like, "Well, you just don't know them like I know them.", or "I don't know what it is, but I just can't stand her.", or "It's a personal thing, and I'd rather not say what it is.", or "It's just something about his spirit that God is showing me. I can't put my finger on it right now." These are signature, classic responses from a person full of the jealous kind of leprosy and who is sent on an assignment by the

69

enemy to come against and hinder the work of other servants in the Body of Christ.

The fact that Miriam was a prophetess did not prevent her from being used by the enemy and being spotted by the flesh. Her case had to be very bad for the hand of God to strike only her out of the three sibling leaders with leprosy. Since Miriam wanted to operate according to her own carnal will, then God gave her what she wanted and caused her to completely be consumed by quick raw flesh all over her entire body. As mentioned above in Song of Solomon 8:6, jealousy is as cruel as the grave which is the ultimate destination and repository of dead things. Like the grave, leprous jealousy wants things dead - it wants reputations dead, ministries dead, churches dead, marriages dead, and even people dead. The spirit of leprosy in operation in this kind of scenario sends the unrighteous on a murder campaign and gives them instructions not to cease until the grave receives a deposit of someone's character, vision, future or life at large. If you have experienced or come across someone (yourself or otherwise) that fits this description, then you or they need a serious cleansing from God. (Psalm 51:10) Just like Miriam, your quest to destroy another person, church, family or ministry will end in your own demise. So stop, take a good Holy Ghost look at yourself and your intentions, and repent before you become consumed like Miriam by your own leprosy.

One could also consider Miriam to be likened to a member of a pastor's family since Moses was the spiritual leader of the people of God. Essentially, you could label her as a pastor's sister. Belonging to a pastor's family does not exempt you from harboring the spirit of leprosy. I come from six generations of pastors on my paternal side of the family and have countless uncles and cousins who pastor - not to mention again the fact that both my father and my brother are bishops. Needless to say, I have experienced a lot which qualifies me to speak regarding pastors' families. Many pastors' families are some of the chief reasons for contention and mess in the church. They can tend to think that the church belongs to them since their relative (father, mother, husband, sibling, etc) is the pastor. They often run the house of God like it is their own house and tend to treat God's sheep abusively thinking that God will not chasten them for their wicked ways. This is a problem across the entire Body of Christ. Who is there to judge us as pastors' kids (PK's), pastor's wives or pastor's siblings? When you stand in a position wherein no one can call you out regarding your unrighteousness or no one can point out your spots and blemishes to advise you to cleanse yourself, then you are like a woman alone in an open field and your virtue is about to be violated by the enemy. You stand in a remote place with no help from the city of counsel nearby (Deuteronomy 22:22 - 27).

King David was blessed to have Nathan, the prophet, who cared about him and feared God enough to carry out the assignment of his prophetic office to confront David. (2 Samuel 12:1 - 14) Nathan pointed out David's sin not to harm or destroy him, but so that David could repent and be reconciled in his relationship with God. Although he was king and could have probably had Nathan beheaded or otherwise executed, David was great enough and wise enough to take heed to Nathan's accusation, humble himself and confess before God. He did not respond like many of us who get offended and almost never speak to the person again, claiming that they are of the devil and against you or your ministry. How leprous and uninformed! Self-righteousness and pride are fleshly blemishes that lead you to think that every positive word spoken about you is true and good, and every negative word is a bad lie. Criticism (even if it comes from an enemy) can help build your character so that you see the areas in you that really do need attention. Beware of people who constantly flatter you with enticing words

71

(Colossians 2:4) to pump up your flesh and increase its leprosy factor. You can not trust a person that only has sweet things to say about you all the time - their sweetness can lead to "truth decay." This is especially true of those who serve in church or ministry leadership roles who are always the target of "suck-ups" who just say things to get on your good side which they feel will set them up for a position. A wise person appreciates constructive correction.

The "Nathans" in the Body of Christ are very rare and scarce. Everybody needs a Nathan that is not afraid of your title or of losing your friendship if they point out your shortcomings and/or those of your friends or family. Nathan keeps you accountable to God. Eli the high priest is the epitome of the downfall and destruction awaiting a spiritual leader who will not correct his family (his sons Hophni and Phinehas who were priests) for sleeping with the women right in the temple and stealing the Lord's offering. (1 Samuel 2:12 - 17) This eventually led to disgrace and the glory of the Lord departing from among them. Eli was a witness to pastors and ministry leaders that an unruly, ungoldly family can harbor the plague of leprosy and ruin a church or ministry.

Not only are pastors' families a target for the spirit of leprosy, but also those that serve closely to ministry leaders. Gehazi (2 Kings 5:20 - 27) was a servant to the prophet Elisha, similar to the function armor bearers serve in today's church. Naaman who was a leper (discussed in detail below) was cured of his leprosy by Elisha and was so thankful that he offered a gift to compensate Elisha for his healing. Demonstrating that you can not buy healing or the things orchestrated by the Spirit of God, Elisha refused to accept the offering. However, his armor bearer Gehazi thought differently and saw dollar signs. After Naaman got on the road to start his journey home, Gehazi runs to catch up with him, cunningly goes behind Elisha's back, and lies to Naaman telling him that Elisha had changed his mind and had requested money to give to some visiting prophets that just arrived at his house. What a lie! His goal was to get money from Naaman for himself. Gifts in those days from someone of Naaman's stature could have amounted to hundreds of thousands of dollars in today's currency. For example, the offering that the Queen of Sheba gave King Solomon while visiting him to see his splendor and David's offering to God for the building of the temple both were worth hundreds of thousands if not millions in today's figures. Therefore, Gehazi probably knew he stood a good chance of garnering a large sum of money by misrepresenting the truth to Naaman on behalf of the prophet of God. Can you imagine the repercussions of lying to a true prophet who discerns things by the Spirit?

When Gehazi returned from getting the money from Naaman through lies and trickery, Elisha asked where he had been. Gehazi then lies again and replies that he had not gone anywhere. This angered Elisha because the Lord showed him by the Spirit what Gehazi had done. As a consequence for his greed and premeditated deception and lies, Elisha pronounced that the same leprosy that was formerly on Naaman would plague Gehazi and his future generations. What a judgment!

Despite the fact that Gehazi served in ministry alongside a powerful man of God, he still suffered from the spirit of greed which led him to lie to get money. Certain opportunities for the church to get money today have awakened that same taste bud of gluttony and greed in the mouths of some of our ministries and churches. It seems that we will do essentially anything and lower our godly standards for a buck, including signing on to government programs that forbid you to use the name of the Lord Jesus where their money is concerned. We are the church of the Lord Jesus Christ, so how is it that we can abandon his name for the sake of a dollar? Some ministries under false pretenses claim in applying for these grants that they will comply with state or local government regulations when it comes to not teaching or influencing the children, youth or other participants towards Jesus, then plan to switch once they receive the funds and violate their contract to do as they please. Either way, it is deception birthed out of greed. The church is founded upon the death, burial and resurrection of Jesus Christ. Therefore, we can not "X" him out of anything that we do. He must remain first in our Christian programs, Christian schools, Christian daycares, Christian television, etc. Otherwise, we are just like the rest of society that offers no Jesus. Jesus is and will always be the answer, and He promised to supply all the needs of His church. (Philippians 4:19)

The church at large has become far too materialistic and overly focused on prosperity, houses, cars, etc. Granted, prosperity does have its place and is important to an extent, but we must remain balanced and also prosper spiritually, not forgetting the purpose for our existence. Money should not be the primary reason for our church services. We must be careful with our building fund drives, conferences, revivals, etc. that they are not *only* designed to raise money and that our quest for money does not eclipse the fact that we come together to worship the Lord, fellowship with and edify the saints, save the lost *and* bring an offering to God. Money must not be our *raison d'etre* or reason for being. Once the people of God experience the presence of the Lord during ministry events, their hearts become willing to give to the Lord and there will be an overflow of proceeds to support the work according to Exodus 35:21, 22a, 29; 36:6, 7:

> And they came, every one whose heart stirred him up, and every one whom his spirit made willing, and they brought the Lord's offering to the work of the tabernacle of the congregation, and for all his service, and for the holy garments. And they came

both men and women, as many as were willing
hearted...The children of Israel brought a willing
offering unto the Lord, every man and woman,
whose heart made them willing to bring for all
manner of work, which the Lord had commanded
to be made by the hand of Moses...And Moses
gave commandment, and they caused it to be pro-
claimed throughout the camp, saying, Let neither
man nor woman make any more work for the offering of the sanctuary. So the people were restrained
from bringing. For the stuff they had was sufficient
for all the work to make it, and too much.

The offering that the children of Israel gave was so over-
abundant that Moses had to literally stop them from giving
because it became too much! Wouldn't you love for your
church or ministry to be in this position where the financial
blessings in the offerings are such that you do not have room
enough to receive it all? (Malachi 3:10) This passage
demonstrates to us that God moves on the hearts of His people to provide for the work of ministry - even to the point of
overflow. It is imperative therefore that we as preachers who
raise or conduct offerings not deceive the people to believe
a promise that God has not spoken. The spirit of leprosy
birthed out of carnal greed causes some of today's ministers
to "prophelie" empty promises to God's sheep in order to
persuade them to get in $1000, $500, and $100 offering
lines. Do not get me wrong, the Lord has moved and con-
tinues to move in offerings by the prophetic - I have experienced MAJOR blessings many times through this kind of
move of God during ministry offerings. You will find this all
throughout the books of Exodus, Leviticus, Numbers, etc.
where the Lord requires the people to bring a certain offering to Him. But I am speaking of the false prophesies associated with these offerings when men and women of God in

the spirit of Gehazi use gimmicks, trickery, and lies to get money from the people. God has enough tithers and other wealthy or simply willing-hearted people positioned in his kingdom to finance the work of His ministry. He has not called us to be like Gehazi and come out of place with God to carnally chase after a dollar when the cattle on a thousand hills belong to Him. (Psalm 50:10)

If you have made money your top priority to the point that you have developed a lustful love relationship with it (1 Timothy 6:10) similar to the case of Gehazi, then greed has opened the door to the plague of leprosy on you, your church or your ministry. It will be the case that your church or ministry's money-hunger will never be satisfied and you will forever be on a mad chase, consumed with trying to get yet another dollar by lying, trickery and gimmicks. In short, we need to shine the light of the Word on our own hearts to inspect and make sure that we are not spotted by greed and gluttony.

Having said that, allow me to further expound on Naaman. Naaman was captain of the Syrian army and a great man, well-regarded in the eyes of the king of Syria. Through him, many battles were won. The Bible says in 2 Kings 5:1,

...he was a mighty man of valor, but he was a leper.

The scriptures do not tell how Naaman contracted leprosy, but his was apparently a mild case in its early stages because he was still intermingling with people and had not been quarantined to prevent the spread of his infectious disease. There was a young Israelite girl whom Syria had taken captive during the war and who served Naaman's wife. Fortunately, this young girl informed Naaman of the prophet Elisha who could cure his leprosy. Through a series of events, Naaman traveled to Samaria and came directly to Elisha's house to be cured of his infirmity, but Elisha refused to see him. Instead, the Bible says in 2 Kings 5:10,

> And Elisha sent a messenger unto him [Naaman],
> saying, Go and wash in Jordan seven times, and
> thy flesh shall come again to thee, and thou shalt
> be clean.

Naaman got angry with Elisha for two reasons: 1) because Elisha would not come out of his house to deal with him directly and call on God in a dramatic display all because Naaman was a man of great status, and 2) because he felt degraded that Elisha instructed him to wash in the Jordan which was such a dirty, muddy river. He felt that there were cleaner rivers or other, more dignified means overall by which a man of his rank should be healed. Naaman's case is a mirror image of many of us in the church. We want answers from the Lord through the man or woman of God, but we seldom want to do what it takes to receive. Like many of us, Naaman was too high minded because of his position to find those instructions appropriate for him. True deliverance is never comfortable and can get ugly.

Although Naaman was a mighty man of valor, had accomplished great military victories, and was highly regarded by his superior, he was still a leper. Somewhere along the way during all of his great exploits, leprosy snuck up and got a hold of him. This is one key reason why we must constantly examine ourselves (Psalm 26:2, 2 Corinthians 13:5) as we go from height to height, from victory to victory, and from glory to glory to make sure that leprosy does not catch us with our hearts and spirits unguarded. James says, "Guard your hearts..." We tend to think that our hearts are clean before God simply because we do all that we do to serve the Lord Jesus in ministry. Not so. This is what I call the typical "Martha mentality" (Luke 10:38 - 42) where we become so busy working *for* God that we really forget all about our relationship *with* God. This leaves an open door for the enemy. We become prayerless and stop consecrating - the beginning stages of leprosy. According to 1 Samuel 12:23, prayerlessness is sin.

However, you are still among the people (like Naaman) and functioning well, but your spirit man is getting further and further away from God. Before you know it, you are lukewarm in your heart while still serving and functioning in the work of ministry. This is the kind of leprosy that slowly builds up on you. This aspect of leprosy does not knock you over the head with a two-by-four because the enemy's intent is to slowly gain momentum on you so that after awhile you will find yourself leprous. Over time you will see spots and blemishes, but the disease had set in a while ago. These come from the "little sins" like slothfulness, not paying your tithes, becoming overly busy with no time to study the Word of God for spiritual strength, etc. Do you find that your success in ministry keeps you so preoccupied that you have little or no time for prayer? After you preach a powerful message that really blesses the people and they compliment you on how well you ministered, do you pluck your lapel and steal God's glory when it does not belong to you? Is it the case that you started out hosting conferences and other ministry events to exalt the name of the Lord Jesus, and somewhere along the way your goal has become to make a name for yourself? Since you have been heading your women's ministry, has it turned out that you have become dominant, high-minded, controlling and haughty? Then the spirit of leprosy has crept up on you as these are the kinds of fleshly, self-motivated spots that prove its presence. The undiscerning rarely notices this kind of leprosy because it is not among the so-called high-category sins like hatred, murder, homosexuality, fornication, etc. We rank sins and give them degrees of evil; but the Bible says in 1 John 5:17 that all unrighteousness, whether big or small to us, is sin. That is why the enemy catches many of us with our shields down and our hearts unguarded. Like Naaman, you need to take a dip in the water of the Word to cleanse you from the beginning stages of what can end up completely consuming you.

Remember, anybody can get leprosy - no matter how important or insignificant you think you are. Satan works at all angles to maximize the number of leprosy-stricken casualties in the church so that the army of God will be wounded and ineffective. We must therefore check ourselves along the ladder of ministry success to ensure that there is no quick raw flesh in the rising. If this segment has revealed some ugly things about you that have convicted you, then you need to rejoice because God is doing a work in you to clean you up to be used in a greater dimension for His divine glory in this end time!

Chapter 6

Garments Spotted By The Flesh

Truth Symptom #6:
~ Leprosy could spread into the leper's garments ~

"...if the plague be spread in the garment...the
plague is a fretting leprosy; it is unclean."
Leviticus 13:51

When leprosy would progress severely, the infected spots in the skin would begin to spread into the garments of the leper. The Bible says that in this case the condition is serious to the point that it is a "fretting" (corroding, bitter, or eroding) leprosy. The plague of leprosy at this stage was aggressive in eroding and eating away at the fabric of the garments the leper wore.

In scripture, a person's garments distinguished their title, position, or the state of their lives; therefore their garments were a powerful statement of their authority or circumstances. Reference is made to various types of garments in the Bible. There were priestly garments (Exodus 28) which Aaron and his descendants were to wear while ministering in their office in the tabernacle or temple. There were also kingly garments (2 Samuel 6:14) or robes that the kings wore in honor of their royal highness and earthly sovereignty. It was these garments that King David danced out of, disrobing himself of his royal supremacy while praising and rejoicing before the Lord over the return of the ark of the covenant. In essence, David took off his garment of kingship and spiritually put on the powerful garment of praise. Widow's garments (Genesis 38:14) were another kind of clothing worn to denote a woman's state of mourning over the loss of her husband. Lastly, there were wedding garments (Matthew 22:11, 12) that were granted typically by high status bridegrooms to all the guests attending their wedding feasts to match their attire with the decor of the festivities and to display the splendor of their wealth. One's garments actually revealed a lot about your identity and status.

Even today, your garments or the clothes you wear make a statement about you. This is where the concept of making a "fashion statement" derived. What message is my attire sending out about me? Does what I wear on the outside accurately reflect who I am on the inside? It would be very difficult for me to dress like society's typical image of a prostitute and, at the same time, convince people that I am really a Catholic nun. In this case, my attire would directly contradict my true identity because the traditional nun's apparel is very distinct and easily recognizable. One's garments advertise who we really are. It is like the sign on the merchant's window that announces what is available inside the store. In fact, the priests' garments were so important that God Himself designed these garments which were highly detailed to represent the priest's responsibility in his intercessory function between God and His people - their duty to minister to God and to the people. His garments visibly distinguished him and were a constant reminder that he was consecrated as holy unto the Lord and ordained to serve in the office of the priesthood. The Bible describes God's design of the priests' garments in fine detail in Exodus chapter 28. We will not expound on all the priests' attire, but specifically, Exodus 28:1, 2, 4 generally recounts God's instruction to Moses regarding the design of the priests' garments where He says,

> And take thou unto thee Aaron thy brother, and his sons with him, from among the children of Israel, that he may minister unto me in the priest's office, even Aaron, Nadab and Abihu, Eleazar and Ithamar, Aaron's sons. And thou shalt make holy garments for Aaron thy brother for glory and for beauty...And these are the garments which they shall make; a breastplate, and an ephod, and a robe, and an embroidered coat, a miter, and a girdle: and they shall make holy garments for Aaron thy brother, and his sons, that he may minister unto Me in the priest's office.

In essence, Jehovah God dressed the priests Himself. What an awe-inspiring thought for the God of the universe to create garments just for you according to His own pattern! Among the several garments that God dressed them in included a breastplate which foreshadowed the breastplate of righteousness spoken of in Ephesians 6:14. It was to guard their hearts from evil so that they would make the right decisions because sin originates in the heart according to Matthew 15:19. There was the mitre or turban for the head which was symbolic of the helmet of salvation. (Ephesians 6:17) The mitre had a gold plate on it with the inscription "Holiness To The Lord" which meant that their minds, logic, reasoning and thought-life were consecrated and dedicated for the Master's use. Further, the salvation of the Lord keeps my soulish man covered by sanctification. God also dressed them in a girdle or sash which is also spoken of in Ephesians 6:14 where Paul talks about having your loins "girt about" or girdled with truth. This girdle was like a belt that was tied around the waist of the priest and was therefore also called the belt of truth, which represented the binding of the Word of truth to their bellies - the center of gravity of the body. The garments that God made were so powerful in what they represented that the Bible records that when the Lord sent fire from heaven to consume and kill Nadab and Abihu for offering up strange fire in their sacrifices - ministering to the Lord in their own way instead of how He commanded - the scripture says in Leviticus 10:5 that their lifeless bodies were carried outside the camp while still in their tunics or priestly garments. In other words, Nadab and Abihu were destroyed by the fire of God's wrath, but this same fire left their garments intact and untouched. How powerful!

Although Nadab and Abihu's ending was not good, there is a divine principle embedded in the durability of their garments to stand in the fire. David said in Psalm 132:9a, "Let thy priests be clothed with righteousness." In other words, the priests' garments generally represented the righteousness and holiness of the Lord in various ways. In addition, Hebrews 12:29 says, "For our God is a consuming fire.", and Exodus 19:18 says regarding Mount Sinai that "...the Lord descended upon it in fire..." Therefore, the fire that came down from heaven was the actual presence of God. Since God is One, then there is only one fire of God that comes from heaven. He does not have various kinds of fire for different situations - one fire to destroy and one fire to purify. There is one fire that comes from God and it consumes everything it touches. So, the fire that came to consume Nadab and Abihu was the same fire of God that consumed the sacrifices offered the right way according to God's commandments. The true fire of God purifies the gold (what is righteous, holy and divine), silver and other durable precious metals and destroys the dross which is symbolic of that that is unrighteous, carnal, or ungodly. (Proverbs 25:4, 2 Timothy 2:20, 21, and 1 Corinthians 3:10 - 15) Because their disobedience deemed them unrighteous before the Lord, the fire of God destroyed Nadab and Abihu, but left their garments untouched.

When you are clothed in righteousness and the fire of tribulation comes to consume you, then as long as you are dressed properly in the spirit, your righteousness will remain steadfast and the trial will not destroy your consecration to and relationship with God. However, if every fiery trial that comes your way pulls you away from God and closer to sin and destruction, then you need to check your garments because you may not be wearing the robe of righteousness that God bestows upon His children. Nervous breakdowns, depression, chronic insomnia from worry, suicidal tendencies, crippling fear, paranoia, etc. - these are among the many symptoms that indicate that your garments are corroding and are being eaten away. Leprosy is somewhere on your garments. James 5:2 says that "...your garments are motheaten" by unrighteousness and people right in the church suffer from these and many more symptoms not mentioned here. Somewhere along the way your garments have become tainted and spotted - no matter how much you speak in tongues, dance, and serve in the church. There is in fact something desperately wrong with your garments. Therefore, you seriously need to check your level of righteousness because the garments that the Father covers us with are durable enough to not only withstand the fire without destruction but also purify us and make us better in the process.

Hence, the priests' natural garments foreshadowed the spiritual garments in which God clothes His church today. Once we are born again and become true children of God, our heavenly Father takes away our spiritual filthy garments symbolic of the uncleanness of our sinful hearts and the iniquity of our ways while living under Satan's influence and control. He then clothes us with the garments of salvation and righteousness. Isaiah 61:10 recounts the prophet rejoicing over the salvation of the Lord where he says,

> I will greatly rejoice in the Lord, my soul shall be joyful in my God; for he hath clothed me with garments of salvation, he hath covered me with the robe of righteousness, as a bridegroom decketh himself with ornaments, and as a bride adorneth herself with her jewels.

Solomon also bears witness when he says, "...let thy priests be clothed with salvation, and let thy saints rejoice in goodness." (2 Chronicles 6:41b) Further, Job in his affliction says, "I put on righteousness and it clothed me..." (Job 29:14a) If you are truly saved and remember what you were before the Lord saved you and if you recall all the dirt you were caught up in and got yourself into during your reckless life of sin, then you too like Isaiah and Solomon would greatly rejoice over God bringing you out of darkness. Some of us were drug dealers, murderers, homosexuals, fornicators, embezzlers, prostitutes, thieves, robbers, habitual liars, gamblers, etc. - but God cleaned us up and made us new (2 Corinthians 5:17). Our Father redeemed us from some things we will never tell anybody about because of how low-grade, unclean and wicked they were. Whenever I get a flashback of where I come from and what I could have been yoked up in today, my soul can not help but rejoice in the God of my salvation.

Once we commit our lives to Him through salvation, our Father dresses His children with holy garments with the intent that we remain clean; and He keeps us clean through the Word of truth. In fact, Jesus said, "Now ye are clean through the Word..." (John 15:3) God dresses us for His own divine glory and rejoices in the fact that He Himself by His own hand grooms us in holiness and righteousness. The Father is not like some parents who could care less about their children's appearance and will take them outside the house looking any kind of way. Their children are often unkept, constantly wearing dirty deteriorating clothes, have wild or uncombed hair, unbrushed teeth, wear muddy socks, and have an odor about them because they have not been bathed for long periods of time. However, we are well kept by the Holy Ghost. In fact, we used to pray in the old church, "Lord, keep me even when I don't wanna be kept." We stored up prayers in advance like Solomon did when he dedicated the temple (1 Kings 8:22 - 61) because we knew that times would come when our flesh would want to stray from God. So we prayed in advance to be kept clean by the power of God. You should do the same today, praying, "When my flesh feels like fornicating, Lord keep me." "When my flesh wants to cuss somebody out, Lord keep me." "When my flesh wants to lie, Lord keep me." "When my flesh reminisces the taste of cocaine back in my mouth, Lord keep me." "When I want to get involved illegal business deals, Lord keep me." "When my flesh wants to harm someone physically, Lord keep me." "When my flesh wants to commit murder - with my tongue or even physical murder, Lord keep me." "When the spirit of suicide comes upon me, Lord keep me."

God promised to keep us clean (2 Thessalonians 3:3, Philippians 4:7), and any good mother or father will also do whatever it takes to keep their children clean and well dressed because they love them and this reflects on the parents. For example, when a parent bathes their child, grooming and getting them ready for a special event, it is quite frustrating to find that your child gets his or her beautiful clothes spotted and wrinkled before you can even leave for the event. Especially on Easter, many try their best to keep their children's little hands away from anything dirty or otherwise that can smear on their fresh, neat little garments.

Anytime they get a little spot, particularly on white clothes, we quickly get a rag and wipe it clean before the stain can set in. Well, when God the Father saved us, He also well groomed us in white fine linen getting us ready for a special event. Revelation 19:8 says regarding the church,

> And to her was granted that she should be arrayed
> in fine linen, clean and white: for the fine linen is
> the righteousness of saints.

John said in Revelation that God arrayed us in fine linen, clean and white which represents our righteousness. Here is another account of how God clothed us in pure white to be spotless. Solomon admonishes us wisely when he says, "Let thy garments be always white..." (Ecclesiastes 9:8) In other words, he is saying, "Don't get your clothes dirty. Stay clean in preparation for this special event." But the problem with the church is that we like small children dressed for a grand occasion keep touching unclean things and getting ourselves into stuff that gets our clothes dirty. We keep spotting and wrinkling our garments. Jude 23 speaks of "the garment spotted by the flesh." This frustrates the Father because every time He turns around (figuratively speaking because the eyes of the Lord are in every place - Proverbs 15:3), we have gotten our hands in deceit and lies, adultery, rebellion, competition, waywardness, hatred, fraud and embezzlement, alcoholism, jealousy, drug addiction, gambling, etc. - the same carnal dirt we just reminisced about above that He brought us out of and cleaned us up from. And this is happening right in the church - from the pulpit to the pews. In many churches across Christendom, particularly in the United States, the saints are swapping husbands and wives, exchanging them like we trade in cars as if God has turned a deaf ear and as if Matthew 5:31, 32 and 1 Corinthians 7 do not exist. Leprosy has hit us hard in this area because this has become commonplace and the divorce rate (nearly 60%) is reportedly higher in the church than in the world. Why? Leprosy has spread into our garments and contaminated our righteousness to the point that we think this is okay because everybody is doing it. Like Nadab and Abihu, we have chosen to handle marriage our own way instead of God's way, which has resulted in hundreds of thousands if not millions of casualties along the way. Whenever a marriage is led by God, divorce is absolutely impossible. But it takes two to make a marriage work, and when it breaks down and ends in divorce, somebody had spiritual leprosy causing their spouse and children much pain and grief.

Many of us women are so desperate for a husband in the church that we will take anything walking - whether jobless, teethless, no arms or legs. Many of us do not seem to care at all whether he is even saved or not, just as long as we have someone to lay down with at night. Quick raw flesh is calling! We must stop marrying just any man that comes along and learn to wait on God. Men used to sweet-talk a woman to get her to marry him, but now all he has to do is show up and she will say, "I do." And these are the kinds of relationships that typically do not last. Leprous flesh has spotted, dirtied, and blemished our clean white linen garment that God Himself dressed us in. We have become tainted by carnality to become self righteousness. Outside of God's righteousness, the Bible says in Isaiah 64:6

> But we are all as an unclean thing, and all our righteousnesses are as filthy rags; and we all do fade as a leaf; and our iniquities, like the wind, have taken us away.

Again, like Nadab and Abihu, we serve in the church and live before God according to our own righteousness which Isaiah declares to be as filthy rags. There has now become a fine line between holy and unholy, between clean and unclean and we have persuaded ourselves to believe that instead of wearing white to our special event like the Father requires, that God will accept us wearing off-white or even beige. Off-white constitutes an off-righteousness which is nothing less than white garments spotted by the spirit of leprosy.

You may ask, "What is the occasion that we are dressed for? What is this special event?" Well, this event is the *marriage supper of the Lamb.* This takes place after Jesus raptures up His church, His Bride out the world to live with Him forever in glory. You may not hear it preached much across the Body of Christ today, but JESUS IS COMING SOON! This was always preached in the old church, but God has sent some preachers to the church today to fore-warn us that the Bridegroom is indeed coming to get His Bride, and we as the church must get our souls right with God and wash our filthy garments to rid them of leprosy. We must remember that the premier type that God uses in the Bible to symbolize the relationship between Christ and His church is the marriage between a husband and a wife. This is why the enemy has attacked us hard so that we no longer value and appreciate the institution of marriage which is to serve as a constant reminder of the love rela-tionship that Christ has with His church. Marriage is so significant that it was the first institution established by God in Genesis, the first miracle Jesus performed was at a wedding ceremony, and the culmination of the church's espousal to Christ is this grand occasion - the marriage supper of the Lamb.

As mentioned in the beginning of this chapter, the Bible speaks of wedding garments that were granted typically by high status bridegrooms to all the guests attending their wedding feasts to match their attire with the decor of the fes-tivities and to display the splendor of their wealth. Because Jesus is the King of kings, sovereign Ruler of the world, and

the Most Royal Highness, He has distributed wedding garments in preparation for His marriage ceremony as well.
Jesus said in Matthew 22:11 - 12,

> And when the King came in to see the guests, he
> saw there a man which had not on a wedding gar-
> ment; and He saith unto him, Friend how camest
> thou in hither not having a wedding garment? He
> was speechless. Then said the King to the ser-
> vants, Bind him hand and foot, and take him away,
> and cast him into outer darkness, there shall be
> weeping and gnashing of teeth. For many are
> called, but few are chosen

This is clearly speaking of the end time marriage supper
of the Lamb and we must be properly clothed in the wedding
garments given to us by the Bridegroom. We can not come
to His marriage supper in our own man-made garments spotted with leprosy, but we must be like the five wise virgins
who prepared themselves for the coming of the Bridegroom
(Matthew 25:1 - 13). Revelation 19:7, 9a says,

> Let us be glad and rejoice, and give honour to
> Him: for the marriage of the Lamb is come, and
> His wife hath made herself ready...And He saith
> unto me, Write, Blessed are they which are called
> unto the marriage supper of the Lamb...

John further recounts in Revelation 7:13, 14,

> And one of the elders answered, saying unto me,
> What are these which are arrayed in white robes?
> And when came they? And I said unto him, Sir
> thou knowest. And he said to me, These are they
> which came out of great tribulation, and have

washed their robes, and made them white in the blood of the Lamb.

Although there are varying theological explanations of what the "great tribulation" actually refers to (some believing it to be the suffering of believers throughout the ages; while others believe there is a specific time of intense tribulation for the saints yet to come), whatever school of thought you subscribe to, the point the scripture is making here is that these believers have come through times of suffering and have washed their robes of righteousness in the blood of the Lamb. The question then becomes this: Why would they have to wash their robes if they were white when they received them from God? Apparently, they had become tainted or spotted during their walk with the Lord, but they were wise enough to come clean before God through the precious blood of Jesus to prepare for the marriage supper of the Lamb. If through reading this chapter you have found areas in your life that have caused your garments to become spotted by the flesh, motheaten and contaminated with the plague of leprosy, then there is much reason for you to rejoice because God has sent a specific Word to you beckoning you to get clean. Jesus is on His way to get His Bride and is about to use you like never before to help get the church ready for His return. With clean garments, your preach will be more heavily anointed than ever before, your prophetic flow will be keener than you have ever experienced, your teaching will be more robust and astounding to others, your church or ministry will go to new heights and experience greater glory, and your personal life will be transformed forever.

Zechariah 3:1 - 5 renders a powerful representation of how God is willing to clean us anew as a royal priesthood and take away our filthy garments - no matter what we have done. God stands ready to rebuke the devil off of your life and take you on a journey to power where the adversary will never be able to touch you again. In Zechariah's vision, although Joshua was a high priest, he still had on filthy garments. But God was gracious, merciful, and loving enough to stay the hand of the enemy and reclothe Joshua, restoring him to his original office and purpose. If you are a pastor, deacon, evangelist, bishop, prophet, teacher, usher, junior missionary, tape ministry head, men's ministry leader, armor bearer, ministry security staff - whatever your position or role in the church or if you are simply a pew member and have fallen from grace into sin and have lost your place in God, even your position in the church, do not be dismayed because God can restore you as he did Joshua the high priest, bestowing even greater honor upon you because of your humility to repent and get clean. Further, we all must do as those in Jerusalem when Jesus entered the city on a donkey the week prior to His crucifixion and resurrection (what we call Palm Sunday today). Matthew 21:8 declares that "a very great multitude spread their garments in the way" for Jesus to walk on, symbolic of the fact that when the presence of the Lord Jesus truly comes, the people must lay down their own righteousness and make it subject to the righteousness of God in Christ.

Scripture says, "...Blessed is he that watcheth, and keepeth his garments..." (Rev. 16:15) So we must therefore ask ourselves on a continual basis, "Am watching over my garments to ensure that they are well kept? Am I properly dressed to meet Jesus when He comes?" "Are my garments motheaten or spotted by any quick raw flesh?" "Has the spirit of leprosy plagued my robe of righteousness?" "Are there any hidden things in my heart that render me unclean and leprous?" As we walk circumspectly and constantly do a maintenance self check instead of pointing the finger at everybody else, we are sure to walk in victory and become clean before God.

Chapter 7

Leprosy In The House

Truth Symptom #7:
~ Leprosy could plague a house and get inside
the walls and structure~

."..behold, if the plague be spread in the house,
it is a fretting leprosy in the house: it is unclean."
Leviticus 14:44

*T*he church is about to embark upon one of the greatest moves of God in its history. If you have any spiritual discernment at all, you can sense a pulsating in the Spirit and recognize that God is up to something. A hunger and a thirst after righteousness have welled up in the serious seekers who want God at any cost and are willing to die to the flesh to have more of Him. There is a remnant of blood-bought children of God, kings and priests, who are determined and willing to hear and obey God, executing His commandments speedily. Those who have a real relationship with the Lord and are connected in the Spirit are aware that what is ensuing is no small matter by any means and are poised in anticipation of this forthcoming wind of the Almighty. We may not know exactly what is on the way, but we know nonetheless that something powerful is coming. The Lord is raising up those with the spirit of Moses to lead the church out of our state of aimless wandering and into this next realm of promise where the kingdom of God will be manifest through the true sons and daughters of Zion and the miraculous will be commonplace. A mighty global end-time wave of the Spirit is on its way.

However, whenever a major move of God takes place whether in our lives, families, churches or ministries, the Lord always requires that the people of God prepare for the magnitude of what He plans to do in the earth. Anytime the Father gives us a promise, whether it is through a vision, dream, prophecy, revelation by the written Word or whatever means He chooses, the Lord has the pattern of imposing a waiting period before He releases the manifestation of what He promised. The book of Leviticus recounts how God takes the children of Israel through a type of holding period on their journey to their promise. Moses and the children of Israel had already left Egypt and were camped for two years at the foot of Mount Sinai before crossing over into Canaan, the land God had covenanted to give their forefathers centuries past. It was here that God pauses to give Israel much instruction about their entire lives concerning their relationship with the Lord Jehovah and with each other that was to govern them when they reached Canaan. He halts their progress just before entering into Canaan and prior to releasing their promise to set some things in order and give them final instruction. Basically, God provides a framework and structure by which they are to prepare to not only embrace the release of their promise but also to maintain their inheritance by establishing order in the camp.

When the time was near that Jesus was to go to the cross, He told His disciples that He was soon to leave them and that where He was going they could not follow Him at that time. But He assured them that they could follow Him later. This dismayed and discouraged the disciples because they had followed Jesus for a total of three and a half years and He was their Rabbi and Lord and they depended heavily upon His guidance. Therefore, to comfort the disciples, Jesus gives them a promise and says in John 14:16 - 18, 26,

> And I will pray the Father, and He shall give you another Comforter, that He may abide with you for ever; Even the Spirit of truth; whom the world cannot receive, because it seeth Him not, neither knoweth Him: but ye know Him; for He dwelleth with you, and shall be in you. I will not leave you comfortless: I will come to you...But the Comforter which is the Holy Ghost, whom the Father will send in My name, He shall teach you all things, and bring all things to your remembrance, whatsoever I have said unto you.

Jesus makes a promise to His disciples that He will send the Comforter or the Holy Ghost. Then He goes on to say in Luke 24:49,

> And, behold, I send the promise of My Father upon you: but tarry ye in the city of Jerusalem, until ye be endued with power from on high.

Then the Bible further says in Acts 1:4 - 5,

> And, [Jesus] being assembled together with them, commanded them that they should not depart from Jerusalem, but wait for the promise of the Father, which, saith He, ye have heard of Me. For John truly baptized with water; but ye shall be baptized with the Holy Ghost not many days hence.

The word *tarry* is derived from the Greek term *kathizo* which means to sit down, to make someone sit down, or to wait. So, what Jesus was saying to His disciples was that although He had promised to send the Holy Ghost, they had to go, sit down and wait in Jerusalem for the release of the power and manifestation of this promise. And it was not until the day of Pentecost (approximately 50 days later) that the promise actually came. The Bible records in Acts 2:1 - 4,

> And when the day of Pentecost was fully come, they were all with one accord in one place. And suddenly there came a sound from heaven as of a rushing mighty wind, and it filled the house where they were sitting. And there appeared unto them cloven tongues like as of fire, and it sat upon each of them. And they were all filled with the Holy Ghost, and began to speak with other tongues, as the Spirit gave them utterance.

The point is that whenever God makes us a promise, His pattern as mentioned before is to place you in a waiting period just like He did the disciples who had to wait for the promise of the Holy Ghost to be released. During your time of waiting or "tarrying," the Spirit of the Lord literally sits you down and pauses some things in your life in order to structure you and your surroundings to accommodate the fullness of the promise so that you will not forfeit what He is about to release. If you read in Acts chapter one you will find that before God sent the promise of the Holy Ghost, the disciples had to structure some things and bring things back in order. Particularly, they had to fill the position that was once held by Judas who betrayed Jesus and later committed suicide. According to God's ordinances, there had to be 12 disciples; so the position that Judas held was filled by Matthias. Having 11 disciples was incomplete because eleven is the number of chaos, disarray and disorder, while 12 is the number of apostolic government and structure. Once Matthias was in position and the 120 were all on one accord, this set things structurally and spiritually in order for the release of the promise.

The Body of Christ is at the point in its history where the Spirit of the Lord is about to release some major promises and prophesies that have been held up for years in order to carry out and facilitate this end-time move of God. As was experienced on the day of Pentecost, the church is in a season where it is about to receive a mighty wind of the Holy Ghost. Again, similar to the case where there were 11 disciples, representing disorder, disarray, and chaos, the church is in a major state of spiritual disorder, and the Spirit of the Lord is calling for the church to restructure and come back into spiritual alignment with God. One of the premier misleading factors about the infirmed condition of the church today is that many of us are actually walking out the manifestation of visions, dreams, and series of prophecies that God gave us in the past. Years ago, the Spirit of the Lord showed you yourself accomplishing great exploits in kingdom building - global evangelistic ministry, pastoring thousands, a heavy prophetic mantle, owning a flourishing business, establishing a successful Christian enterprise, etc. Now much of what we envisioned is coming to pass which leads many to believe that God must be pleased with us because of what we consider to be ministry success. While we have embraced many of these promises, however, we have also recognized at the same time that something is seriously wrong in Canaan. You have tried to identify why your ministry is falling apart; why it is that everything you touch seems to crumble; why the services you lead are not effective; why your conferences and fellowships are dwindling and powerless; why your church will not grow any further; why your revivals do not revive; why it seems as though you have all the church hype and sensationalism but no manifested demonstration of the true glory of God, etc. You have wondered why there is so much tension and bitterness and many blood battles between ministry and auxiliary leaders within your church. Even though you may have a mega church or a world-renown ministry, down in your gut, you know that something is eating away at the foundation. People are leaving your church or ministry in droves and it is on its way to or has already become a has-been religious entity and a fleeting thought in the community. And you are wondering, "What is happening in Canaan?"

Well, could it be the case that you are like the owner of the house depicted in Leviticus 14:35 where he or she says, "...It seemeth to me there is as it were a plague in the house."? Could the plague of leprosy be in your house? Is there any reason why the Spirit of the Lord would chasten your ministry, church, or family? You mean to tell me that God chastens ministries, families, and churches, etc. Yes, absolutely! If the Lord rebuked and chastened the nation of Israel who were His people, then He also chastens the church who are also His people and whom the Bible declares "are a chosen generation, a royal priesthood, an holy nation." (1 Peter 2:9). So God does chastise His people collectively at times because He says, "As many as I love, I rebuke and chasten; be zealous therefore and repent." (Revelation 3:19). In fact, He declared in Deuteronomy 28:58 - 62,

> If thou wilt not observe to do all the words of this law that are written in this book, that thou mayest fear this glorious and fearful name, THE LORD THY GOD; Then the Lord will make thy plagues wonderful, and the plagues of thy seed, even great plagues, and of long continuance, and sore sicknesses, and of long continuance. Moreover he will bring upon thee all the diseases of Egypt, which thou wast afraid of; and they shall cleave unto thee. Also every sickness, and every plague, which is not written in the book of this law, them will the

Lord bring upon thee, until thou be destroyed. And
ye shall be left few in number, whereas ye were as
the stars of heaven for multitude; because thou
wouldest not obey the voice of the Lord thy God.

The Lord was very explicit in forewarning the people of
God of the consequences of disobedience and forsaking His
laws and commandments. Among the children of Israel in
scripture and in the church today, God has followed through
on His Word. The Lord has done exactly what He said in
response to the waywardness of the church and has allowed
the flesh to spot and contaminate the walls of the house. The
Lord loves His children and did not desire that they lose anything that He gave them. You and I both know, however, that
when there are no guidelines in place, people (e.g. the flesh)
tend to go wild. Even with order established, the flesh still
likes to operate according to its own desires. In society today
there are laws of our land and if you violate a law and get
caught, there are repercussions. If you disregard traffic laws
and run a red light, you will get a ticket. If you commit murder, then you will go to jail; and based on the type of murder committed (e.g. manslaughter, first degree, premeditated,
etc.), you could be executed. Similarly, God had to establish
His laws and order among Israel to police the land and maintain holiness. In some cases, based on the degree of the vio-
lation of the laws of the Lord, striking a house with the
plague of leprosy was the judgment. Because leprosy was
such an aggressive and destructive contagion and because
God did not want it to spread and infect the entire camp, the
Lord gave specific instructions to Moses and Aaron on how
to diagnose and deal with leprosy in a house. Leviticus
14:33 - 35, 39b, 40 declares,

And the Lord spake unto Moses and unto Aaron,
saying, when ye come into the land of Canaan,

which I give to you for a possession, and I put the
plague of leprosy in a house of the land of your possession; And he that owneth the house shall come
and tell the priest, saying, It seemeth to me there is
as it were a plague in the house...and, behold, if the
plague be spread in the walls of the house; Then the
priest shall command that they take away the stones
in which the plague is, and they shall cast them into
an unclean place without the city...

Leprosy was so active that it could infect all kinds of
materials - the flesh, garments, and even the walls and structure of a house. Walls in scripture represent the defense and
security from outside intrusion that is provided by a solid
framework and structure. When an enemy sought to overthrow a city, he would attempt to break down its walls and
attack the land. Joshua defeated Jericho by tearing down the
walls of the city. (Joshua 6:20) When your walls become
affected, your defense and security becomes weakened.
Particularly, the walls referred to in our passage above speak
of the plaster connected to the stones that make up the exter-
nal structure of the house. So, leprosy was so destructive
that it could erode through plaster (a mixture of lime, sand
and water) and spread into the stones. And we are those
stones. The Bible refers to us as lively stones where Peter
speaks in 1 Peter 2:5,

Ye also, as lively stones, are built up a spiritual
house, an holy priesthood, to offer up spiritual
sacrifices, acceptable to God by Jesus Christ.

The Bible considers us as the stones that collectively
make up the spiritual house of God. We as individuals and
our churches are all the house of God and leprosy has hit the
walls and stones of the house. Many of our churches have

not fasted in years and consecration is almost a dirty word. Prayer is reserved only for emergencies - like if someone is deathly ill or someone's child gets arrested - you know the serious stuff that we only think we need God for. Holiness is not preached, and many are doing what is right in their own eyes like in the days of Noah. *It seemeth to me as it were a plague in the house.* Sunday School and Bible Study are ghostly empty because people have no real reverence for the power of the Word of God. Saints show up late for service and leave early. Much talking and walking occur during the most strategic time in the service - the altar call or call to discipleship, many of which are weak with no passion to convict and compel the unbeliever to come out of darkness and allow a loving Jesus to loose them from the stronghold of the adversary. In fact, many ministries have no altar calls at all because they have no intention of bringing people to God. But, Jesus commands us to compel sinners to come to Him. (Luke 14:23) When the preached Word comes forth, you find more people outside (smoking cigarettes perhaps) and in the bathrooms than in the sanctuary to be cleansed and instructed by the Word. We have lost our true reverence and fear of the Lord. All this may seem unimportant, but the fact of the matter is that the enemy through the plague of leprosy in the walls is strong at work using these tactics as weapons in his vehement plan to overthrow and defeat the church by its own flesh and carnality.

All across Christendom many have tried to figure out exactly what is wrong with the church, at large. A lull has blanketed the Body of Christ overall, causing us not to have a warrior-like soldier mentality. (Ephesians 6:11 - 17, 2 Timothy 2:3) We are in spiritual warfare, and many have put down our weapons of war, took off our armor, laid down our shields, and have picked up Pina Colada's as if we were at a resort. Every Sabbath, the Spirit of the Lord is blowing the trumpet in Zion calling and assembling His army together to give us our marching orders and military assignment. (Numbers 10:2 - 10, Jeremiah 4:5, Joel 2:15) Church gatherings across Christendom begin chronically late with no intention to meet God on time. If we expect God to move in our midst, then we must have enough decency and reverence to show up at the set time we establish. I remember a time when a sinner wanted to give his life to the Lord and came knocking at about 11:45 a.m. Sunday morning on the doors of a locked, unopened church that had a sign on the front lawn that said, "SUNDAY MORNING WORSHIP SERVICE: 11:00 A.M." What if that was this sinner's last attempt at salvation? This is just one example of many situations wherein people sit out on the parking lot waiting for the church doors to open because the slothful leaders are *always* late. When you are in a battle, you can not be late or missing in action (MIA). We have a lot of Christian MIA's who wear the title of soldier, but are not on their post for war. And the enemy is gaining ground on our territory. However, you must show up at the appointed time dressed for battle and prepared to execute the battle plan given by God through the man or woman of God.

Job says, "Is not there an appointed time to man upon the earth? Are not his days like the days of a hireling?" (Job 7:1) The phrase *appointed time* in scripture is derived from the Hebrew word *tsvaah* which translates to mean *warfare*. In other words, what Job was saying is that man's life is assigned to warfare. From the time we are birthed into the earth, we are entangled in a war and you are automatically enlisted in Satan's armed forces. Once we accept the Lord, then we break rank from the enemy, switch armies and become soldiers of the cross. Many of us were exuberant aggressive militia in the enemy's camp and have now become slack and slothful in the army of the Lord.

The Bible says that we are first natural then spiritual. The Word of the Lord declares in 1 Corinthians 15:46 - 47,

Howbeit that was not first which is spiritual, but that which is natural; and afterward that which is spiritual. The first man is of the earth, earthly: the second man is the Lord from heaven.

In telling parables, Jesus always used natural things to demonstrate a spiritual principle. We are first born in the natural then born-again of the Spirit. If we do not show up for church on time and are always slothful and late for our ministry assignments in the natural, then so it is in the spirit. We are also late in the spirit and miss the timing of God as well. If the enemy can keep a strong slothful grip on our minds when it comes to our natural duties, then lulling us to sleep spiritually is no problem; and the adversary has accomplished this. Satan has deceived us to believe that promptness is unimportant. Our prophecies are months late, and by the time we do get around to delivering the prophetic Word God gave us, the wind of the Spirit has long since spoken it, performed it and moved on to something else. Have you ever had someone to bring you a message that God told them to give you a long, long time ago? I have experienced this on many occasions where people have come to me saying, "God told me to deliver this Word to you a long time ago, but I'm just getting around to it...two years later" By the time they speak the Word to you, your season has shifted and that Word becomes irrelevant. I am guilty as well and have missed God at times by either being late with a prophetic Word or not delivering it at all while still pondering over what to do with the Word I heard. The plague of leprosy keeps us wrapped up in carnal fear, intimation, and pride, causing us not to want to be embarrassed in the event that we are not "on point." We are worried about our reputations, but must become like Jesus and make ourselves of no reputation (Philippians 2:7) and release the prophetic Word God commands at the appointed time - the time that this aspect of the Sword of the Spirit is needed for war.

It is imperative that we recognize that we are God's strategic courier servants who deliver the mail, and the mail is scheduled to and must arrive at the appointed time in the heat of the battle - not when the battle is over. We have become late and slothful soldiers and the Spirit of the Lord is commanding us to WAKE UP! In Joel 3:9, the prophet cries,

> Proclaim ye this among the Gentiles; Prepare war, wake up the mighty men, let all the men of war draw near; let them come up...

Isaiah also heralds in Isaiah 52:1,

> Awake, awake; put on thy strength, O Zion; put on thy beautiful garments, O Jerusalem, the holy city: for henceforth there shall no more come into thee the uncircumcised and the unclean. Shake thyself from the dust; arise, and sit down, O Jerusalem: loose thyself from the bands of thy neck, O captive daughter of Zion.

"WAKE UP! WAKE UP! WAKE UP!" I hear the Spirit of the Lord crying, "WAKE UP CHURCH! WAKE UP! WAKE UP!" The church at large is slumbering and must wake up. It is dangerous to sleep on the battle field. When the woman Jael defeated Sisera (captain of the Canaanite army) during the battle between Israel and Canaan, she used milk as a part of her strategy to kill him. Sisera had fled from Barak (and Deborah) who was winning the war and chasing after him. Sisera ran on foot to Jael's house for safety, and Judges 4:18, 19, 21 recounts,

> And Jael went out to meet Sisera, and said unto him, Turn in, my lord, turn in to me; fear not. And

when he had turned in unto her into the tent, she covered him with a mantle [rug]. And he said to her, Give me, I pray thee, a little water to drink; for I am thirsty. And she opened a bottle of milk, and gave him drink, and covered him...Then Jael Heber's wife took a nail of the tent, and took an hammer in her hand, and went softly unto him, and smote the nail into his temples, and fastened it to the ground: for he was *fast asleep* and weary. So he died.

Why would Jael give Sisera milk instead of water? She gave the enemy milk because it contains a substance called tryptophan that causes you to sleep. This is why we give small children warm milk before bedtime. Her intention was to lull him to sleep so that she could kill him by driving a tent nail through his head and defeat him. God always operates in three dimensions. There is the Outer Court which is the place of the flesh where we drink spiritual milk. There is the Inner Court which is the place of the soulish realm or mind where we eat spiritual bread. And there is the Holy of Holies which is place of the spirit where we eat the meat of the Word. The church is still in the Outer Court which is the place of the flesh where all you can handle is the milk of the Word because we are spiritual babies. (Hebrews 5:12 - 14) Let me remind you that the only thing that early stage babies do is *drink milk and sleep.* Outer court flesh has us yoked up and jeopardized us into sleeping our way to destruction. If you head an auxiliary, church, or ministry that has fallen asleep on the battle field, then I can assure you that there have been casualties because the enemy has never gone to sleep and has been attacking you, your family, and church while you have been snoring like Sisera. We must get this leprosy out of the walls and structure of the house.

Chronic slothfulness, lack of prayer, no consecration -

these are the obvious streaks of leprosy that plague the walls and structure of the house. However, there are the less noticeable symptoms that threaten to deceive even the elect of God these days. (Matthew 24:24) The truth of the matter is that there is witchcraft in our pulpits. The spirit of wizardry and sorcery abounds in many of our churches. This is a key indicator of a seriously leprous house with contaminated walls. When Moses was sent by God to command Pharoah to let the children of Israel go, Moses performed miracles by the power of God to prove that the Lord had sent Him. However, Pharoah also called his magicians and sorcerers who could mimic those miracles. The scripture says in Exodus 7:8 - 12,

> And the Lord spake unto Moses and unto Aaron, saying, When Pharoah shall speak unto you, saying, Shew a miracle for you: then thou shalt say unto Aaron, Take thy rod, and cast it before Pharoah, and before his servants, and it shall become a serpent. And Moses and Aaron went in unto Pharoah, and they did so as the Lord had commanded: and Aaron cast down his rod before Pharoah, and before his servants, and it became a serpent. Then Pharoah also called the wise men and sorcerers: now the magicians of Egypt, they also did in like manner with their enchantments. For they cast down every man his rod, and they became serpents: but Aaron's rod swallowed up their rods.

How was it possible for Pharoah's magicians to reproduce the miracles manifested by the power of God? It was the spirit of witchcraft and sorcery in operation. The magicians were empowered by evil spirits that can also do tricks and manifest their wicked power in various ways. (Revelation 13:14, 16:14,

19:20) This is the evil side of the spirit realm. Remember that Satan is real, and he has many demons on assignment to deceive the Body of Christ and the world. When the Spirit of the Lord had departed from Saul and he wanted to contact Samuel from the dead for a Word from the Lord, Saul consulted with the witch of Endor, a woman with a familiar spirit, because Saul was separated from God and could not hear the voice of the Lord. (1 Samuel 28:6 - 25) Can you imagine that? Saul, the once-anointed, was trying to use evil means (a familiar spirit) to get a Word from the Lord. This same principle is in operation among us when we use familiar spirits and spirits of divination to accomplish so-called Godly things. You claim that you hear "a Word" in the spirit. You may in fact be hearing something, but my question to you is this: Are you hearing the authentic voice of the Spirit of God or are there demonic spirits in operation in your life. This is nothing new because psychics operate in these spirits everyday which is how they claim to know your future. We also pride ourselves in knowing the unknown which simply amounts to head knowledge and not divine revelation. Therefore many across Christendom have resorted to becoming carnal church psychics trying constantly to predict your future without a Word base to support their witchcraft. Do not be tricked to believe that psychics (church or otherwise) are of God as they can never reveal the mind of Christ to you because they do not know His mind. They do not understand the "hidden manna" (Revelation 2:17) of the gospel because it is particularly hidden from them (1 Corinthians 2), and they are not people of prayer because they do not talk to God - they listen to demons.

Consequently, many of our churches are experiencing serious internal battles. There is definitely a holy war between the righteous and the unrighteous. There is a Mexican stand-off between the holy and the unholy. The problem is that many pastors do not know who is really called of God and who is working for the enemy (whether they themselves know it or not). Many do not recognize that there are witches right on their ministerial staff including evangelists, in-house prophets and prophetesses, teachers, elders, missionaries, and others that carry the gospel and are a part of the structure and walls of the church. These are your church pillars. You have your Moses' and Aarons as well as your magicians and sorcerers within the confines of our church and ministry foundations. These witches are working spiritual magic and sorcery right in the church. They watch those truly called by God very closely, then they try to mimic and reproduce the authentic anointing and the works of the Spirit. If they see Aaron throw down his rod and it becomes a serpent, then the witches throw theirs down and it becomes a serpent. Whenever Moses and Aaron prophesy, then the witches prophesy. When the righteous operate in the miraculous, the witches try to mimic and operate in the miraculous. If you are a present-day Moses or an Aaron, then do not be disheartened or discouraged by the witches because the scriptures say that eventually Aaron's rod swallowed up the rod of the magicians. This means that the hand of the Lord on your life will at the appointed time eclipse and nullify the works of the witches that compete against you. The true prophets are about to rise out of obscurity and overshadow the evil works of the spirit of deception at work in today's propheliars, ungodly evangelists, and witches in the church.

Jesus further proves that the unclean can in fact work miracles and other wonders in Matthew 7:22 - 23 and John reveals it in Revelation 16:14, respectively,

> Many will say to Me in that day, Lord, Lord, have we not prophesied in Thy name? and in Thy name have cast out devils? and in Thy name done many wonderful works? And then I will profess unto them, I never knew you: depart from Me, ye that work iniquity.

For they are the spirits of devils, working miracles, which go forth unto the kings of the earth and
the whole world, to gather them to the battle of
that great day of God Almighty.

Jesus is admonishing us not to be caught up in the working of miracles and other spiritual signs. Do not get hyped
and misguided by the fact that something miraculous
occurred when you ministered because if your spirit and
character do not line up with the Word of God and you are
constantly bearing wicked and evil fruit, then you may be
operating under the power of a demon - right in the church.
The church constantly seeks after signs to prove the hand of
God, just like Pharoah requested a miracle from Moses. We
want spiritual power and signs for fleshly reasons so that we
can claim that we are greater and more spiritual than others.
This is nothing more than fleshly spirituality. What an oxy-
moron! However, Jesus told the carnal scribes and Pharisees
in Matthew 12:39a, "...An evil and adulterous generation
seeketh after a sign..." We have become spotted by our
fleshly desire to see tricks like rabbits out of a hat in the
church. The plague of leprosy is deep in our walls and keeps
us on a mad hunt, constantly seeking after the spectacular
and following after a showy sign of the movement of the
Spirit. Your sign should be in your ability to love and live
holy, not in your ability to prophesy, speak in tongues, lay
hands, or perform magic. Please bear in mind that somebody
is fulfilling the scriptures that Jesus prophesied about when it
comes to evil workings, false prophesies, etc. in the church.
Is it you? The Lord Jesus also said that signs of the miraculous would follow the believer. (Mark 16:17) We have
become so leprous and carnal that we have gotten this thing
totally backwards and have been following after the signs.
Signs will trick you every time because of the witches, sorcerers and magicians in the church. They *can* produce signs.

So stop looking for magic shows and start seeking hard after God. You must hunger for Him, search for Him, and seek Him until you find Him. (Psalm 27:8, 105:4)

Jesus tells you how you can identify the true people of God, His true disciples - not the counterfeits - when he says in Luke 13:35,

> By this shall all men know that ye are my disciples, if ye have love one to another.

Jesus said that Godly love would be your sign in the last days of the true child of God because 1 John 4:8 declares that "He that loveth not knoweth not God; for God is love." Infested across Christendom are a lot of mean, unloving people who claim to know Jesus and who are a part of the walls and structure of the church. These are the same tongue-talking, prophesying, shouting saints who seem to hate the brethren. Jesus used love as the key identifier of His true disciples because He had already prophesied that in the last days "…because iniquity shall abound, the love of many shall wax [grow] cold." (Matthew 24:12) To love someone who despises you is a hard thing if you try to do it in the flesh. To love someone who lies on you and scandalizes your name is also a hard thing if you try to do it in the flesh. And because many of us are reveling in and spotted by the flesh, we simply can not produce genuine love to everybody and not just our friends, family or who we like. That is expressly why we *must* walk after the Spirit and not after the flesh. (Galatians 5:16 - 17) Hence, you may quote scriptures, lay hands on the sick, prophesy, preach, usher, etc., but if the love of God is not in you, then you need to seriously check to see who your true father is because God's children have in them the DNA in their spiritual blood that causes them to love.

Moreover, Christendom has become so "ministry minded" and "churchy" that we are caught up in a whirlwind of over indulging in "religious busy-ness." We host events just to stay busy and keep activity going instead of by the leading of the Lord; and we have over-dosed on conferences. Do not get me wrong, the church does indeed need inspiring events like conferences, revivals, fellowships, workshops, retreats, etc. that enrich and edify us spiritually, facilitating and encouraging a higher level of response to God in sanctification and holiness. Further, we do indeed need occasions wherein we celebrate victories (ministry anniversaries, mortgage burnings, erecting new buildings, etc.) that God bestows upon us and next dimensions that the Lord ushers us to (e.g. ordinations, licensing, ministerial graduations, etc.) In fact, in the book of Leviticus, of the seven feasts the Lord instructs Israel to commemorate, five of them are feasts of celebration for what the Lord had done. So, God commands His people to hold events and celebrations with purpose. Many of our events, however, are without purpose and are rooted in "busy-ness" to simply have something else to do in order not to be idol, for fear of boring the people and losing members, or to keep up and compete with the church or ministry around the corner. And this is why we see so many conferences. Conferences, conferences, conferences! With all these conferences, the world should be saved. Is your conference called of God or are you just caught up in "religious busy-ness?" (Isaiah 1:12 - 15) Do your revivals actually revive the saints, or are they dead services that put one in the mind of the valley of dry bones? Are they simply events scheduled to fill the ministry calendar by the planning committee? It is imperative that we inspect our walls and begin to restructure and bring Godly order to our "busy-ness." If you put God first and do things according to His divine order, then He will grant you good success. (Joshua 1:8)

In addition, many non-pastoring preachers who are members of churches get restless while sitting under the ministry of their pastor. Based on what we consider to be the typical progression up the clerical or religious ladder, these preachers get "the itch" to start a church. Some of these men and women of God go out and start ministries based on their own carnal will and desires (glamour, money, boredom, excitement, power, fame, etc.) without having heard from God at all. There is a true story that a world-renown preacher, teacher and author tells of how he had gone outside of the will of God and started a church that God had not told him to and had pastored this ministry for several years. The church grew to thousands of members, but all along, God had told him that he was not called to be a pastor. This message kept ringing in his heart until one day, he humbled himself, heeded to the voice of God, and turned the ministry over to his son who was actually the one with the pastoral calling on his life. Do not let our concept of ministry success mislead you to think you are on track with God. This is one example of a case of a large church started by a non-pastor, but grew nonetheless. Paul says in 1 Corinthians 3:10 - 15,

> According to the grace of God which is given unto me, as a wise masterbuilder, I have laid the foundation, and another buildeth thereon. But let every man take heed how he buildeth thereupon. For other foundation can no man lay than that is laid, which is Jesus Christ. Now if any man build upon this foundation gold, silver, precious stones, wood, hay, stubble; Every man's work shall be made manifest: for the day shall declare it, because it shall be revealed by fire; and the fire shall try every man's work of what sort it is. If any man's work abide which he hath built thereupon, he shall receive a reward. If any man's work shall be burned, he shall suffer loss: but he himself shall be saved; yet so as by fire.

What the Word of the Lord is saying is that we must be careful not to start churches, ministries, and other works that God has not called us to. Paul says that he was operating and building in the kingdom based on the grace that God gave him to do it. If our works are not built on what the Lord has commanded, then according to the scriptures, we have done them for nought and it will be to God as if we did nothing. Paul says that "the day shall declare it" and try every man's work in the fire to see whether it is a work of gold, silver or other durable metal created by God and will stand in the fire or whether it is a work of wood, hay or stubble which will make a barn fire, burn up and be destroyed. This is the principle in which the song that says, "Only what you do for Christ will last" is rooted. The day that Paul speaks of is the Judgment Seat of Christ where the fire of the Holy Ghost is going to judge the saints, rewarding us for the work that we did that was built upon Jesus Christ (in other words God told you to do it and you did it unto the Lord and not because of your own fleshly desires) and causing us to suffer loss for works we erected and started that God never called or graced us to do. This is where we suffer loss due the reward in heaven that we forfeit and secondarily due to all the time, purpose, destiny, money, effort, etc. we wasted being out of the will of God. Again, for this, there will be no reward, and that will be a major loss.

We need to check to see if our houses are birthed out of carnal fleshy desires to be something God has not called us to be. Ask yourself, "Am I sure God called me to pastor a flock? Do I have the grace to lead this evangelistic ministry or am I just competing with evangelist so-and-so? Are my conferences God-inspired or am I operating on my own leprous vision and going along with the masses? Am I really a bishop or am I just power hungry and lusting after a prestigious title? Is the grace for the bishopric really on my life even though I have failed miserably at pastoring my own 30-member church? It would be a horrendous tragedy to get to heaven and find that, although you yourself are saved and made it to glory to see Jesus, the work you have done on the earth has been for years playing out of bounds which scored you no spiritual points. What a travesty that would be! Like a football player who fouled out a long time ago, running vehemently toward a goal for which he is ineligible due to him being out of bounds, many church leaders and workers are likewise running outside of the perimeters of God's boundaries for their lives. Therefore, we must follow the example of the game of football, and symbolically go back to the place where we were last legitimately in-bounds (in the will of God), discount all of our foul play which has scored us zero points with God, and proceed from there with the intent to stay in the perfect will of the Master. Therefore, to prevent this most dreadful scenario of suffering major loss from actually taking place when we stand before the Judgment Seat, we must examine ourselves and the walls and structure of our spiritual houses (church-wise and individually) to ensure that we did in fact receive a Word of instruction from the Lord for all the "religious busy-ness" that pervades the Body of Christ.

Anytime the Father starts to bring order into a house or situation, then this means that a major thrust of the Spirit is about to break forth. When the Spirit of the Lord took Ezekiel to the valley of dry bones, there was complete disarray among the bones as they were completely dismantled, disconnected and out of order. The case seemed hopeless. But, the Lord commanded the prophet Ezekiel to prophesy to put sinews, flesh, skin, and breath back into these bones. And when the prophetic Word of God was spoken out of the mouth of the prophet, order was restored and the bones became a marching army. The prophet says in Ezekiel 37:10 -11,

> So I prophesied as He commanded me, and the
> breath came into them, and they lived, and stood up

upon their feet, an exceeding great army. Then He said unto me, Son of man, these bones are the whole house of Israel: behold, they say, Our bones are dried, and our hope is lost: we are cut off for our parts. Therefore prophesy and say unto them, Thus saith the Lord God; Behold, O my people, I will open your graves, and cause you to come up out of your graves, and bring you into the land of Israel.

In essence, what the Lord had shown Ezekiel was that once the true prophetic Word of the Lord came forth and began to revive and operate on the dry bones in their dead state of disarray, then order would be brought back to the house of Israel and they would become a great army ready to possess the land. All throughout Ezekiel chapter 37 the scriptures speak of how the wind of God brought a mighty restructuring and revival to the bones, which represented the people of God. If we are to embrace the full measure of this great end-time move of God, we must allow the Spirit of the Lord to sweep through our houses and clean the walls, structure, stones and foundation from the plague of leprosy that is pandemic across the Body of Christ.

Chapter 8

The Leper Pronounced Clean

Truth Symptom #8:
~ When leprosy covered the entire body, the
leper was then pronounced clean ~

"And if a leprosy break out abroad in the skin,
and the leprosy cover all the skin of him that hath the
plague from his head even to his foot, wheresoever
the priest looketh; Then the priest shall consider:
and, behold, if the leprosy have covered all his flesh,
he shall pronounce him clean that hath the plague:
it is all turned white: he is clean."
Leviticus 13:12, 13

*H*ow contradictory this seems! Initially when I read this particular verse, I was a bit confused because it seemed inconsistent and backwards that if a person were spotted with leprosy in different parts of the body, then they were considered unclean, but once leprosy covered the entire body or "all his flesh" then he would be pronounced clean. This verse stood out to me like a sore thumb, seeming to flow countercurrent to the rest of the law of leprosy (Leviticus 14:57b). I therefore sought the Lord for understanding and for Him to make this plain to me because although this appeared a bit odd, I sensed a strong, divine message to the people of God embedded in this specific scripture. You see, there are some things that God will reveal to you openly without you having to do much searching at all; but there are other pearls of divine wisdom that God will cause you to search out and seek for as one who seeks after a treasure in the ocean deep. Because the Body of Christ has become slothful and lazy, we do not make it a practice to dig into the Word of God to find where He has hidden treasures. This is the hidden manna that Jesus speaks of in Revelation 2:17. Isaiah said, "Seek ye out of the book of the Lord, and read..." (Isaiah 34:16a) All that many of us do is *read the Bible* and we basically only do that once in a while. Rarely, however, do we also seek out of God's precious Word. Acts 17:11 speaks of how the Bereans "searched the scriptures daily" to verify that what Paul and Silas had preached was sound and true.

After waiting on God to open me up to the meaning of what He was saying here in His Word, the Spirit of the Lord took me to Isaiah chapter one. What God speaks to Judah and Jerusalem in the first chapter of Isaiah is a mirror image and complete parallel of what the Word of the Lord spoke regarding leprosy in Leviticus 13:12, 13 and is a most revealing and powerful promise and warning from God to His people. Isaiah 1:1 - 6 says,

> The vision of Isaiah the son of Amoz, which he saw concerning Judah and Jerusalem in the days of Uzziah, Jotham, Ahaz, and Hezekiah, kings of Judah. Hear, O heavens, and give ear, O earth: for the Lord hath spoken, I have nourished and brought up children, and they have rebelled against me. The ox knoweth his owner, and the ass his master's crib: but Israel doth not know, My people doth not consider. Ah sinful nation, a people laden with iniquity, a seed of evildoers, children that are cor-

rupters: they have forsaken the Lord, they have provoked the Holy One of Israel unto anger, they are gone away backward. Why should ye be stricken any more? ye will revolt more and more: the whole head is sick, and the whole heart faint. From the sole of the foot even unto the head there is no soundness in it; but wounds, and bruises, and putrifying sores: they have not been closed, neither bound up, neither mollified with ointment.

The Lord is saying to Judah and Jerusalem that they have rebelled so much against Him that they are worse off than the ox and the ass. God says the ox knows his owner and the ass knows his master's crib (or manger), but Israel did not even know or consider their God. The Spirit of the Lord goes on to say that the people were so full of sin and iniquity and had gone so astray and backwards that they provoked the Lord to anger to the point that He asks, " Why should ye be stricken anymore?" with judgments and plagues. Why should He continue to inflict and strike them with leprosy and other diseases when it does them no good? They only rebel more and indulge in greater sins and wickedness. It was like chastising a child who only got worse with each punishment or whipping. Since the punishment is intended to result in repentance and obedience, the parent then out of both love and frustration considers further chastisement a waste and decides to no longer discipline the child in the same manner because the child's behavior gets no better. This was the scenario between God and Israel (i.e. Judah and Jerusalem) and is the same state of the church today. We have been chastened and chastened and chastened by our Father to encourage us to get ourselves right with God as a whole, but these spiritual whippings have not turned us to repentance because we are still head-strong in disobedience, waywardness, and rebellion and refuse to fall on our faces and surrender to the hand of the Almighty. Marital breakdown is at an all time high; greed and lying is the order of the day among us; competition and church politics between leaders abound, organizations break off and dissolve and new ones start almost every month because so many pastors want to be bishops; the sheep are frustrated and confused by the instability of our organizations; racism is still much alive; many of our music ministries are full of sexual sin, pride and haughtiness which hampers the true flow of the Spirit; there is no real church growth, only membership transfer with the people of God running from church to church; sinners mock and sneer at our pastors and the church overall because they know of our mess and do not want to come out of sin in the world and into sin in the church; the saints do not know the Bible and prayer is almost a curse word in the Body of Christ; physical sickness and disease have infested our natural bodies; and much, much more. [These issues have been mentioned before but bear repeating to illustrate a point.] Can you see the heavy hand of chastisement that has been on us as a result of the plague of leprosy that God has allowed to hit the church? Can you see how messed up we are? Can you see yourself? Can you see how this mode of chastisement is not working to make us better in our hearts? Now, can you see why God would choose to no longer discipline us in this way anymore?

As the Lord spoke concerning Israel through the prophet Isaiah, the church is likewise sick in the head and afflicted in the heart, and from head to foot is unsound and full of wounds, bruises and sores from the punishment of the plague of leprosy and other diseases. This is a clear diagnosis of the Body of Christ today which is completely parallel and identical to the foreshadow of what God declared in Leviticus 13:12 where He says, "...if the leprosy break out abroad in the skin, and the leprosy cover all the skin of him that hath the plague from his head even to his foot, wheresoever the priest looketh..." Everywhere you looked, the plague of leprosy had hit the house of Israel (meaning Judah and Jerusalem) as a result of their sin and has similarly struck the church hard and has afflicted us from head to foot - from pastors and leaders to pew members.

The Lord goes on to depict how leprosy had inflicted the people symbolically from head to foot, causing even their land to be affected and attacked in Isaiah 1:7 - 15 where He says,

> Your country is desolate, your cities are burned with fire: your land, strangers devour it in your presence, and it is desolate, as overthrown by strangers. And the daughter of Zion is left as a cottage in a vineyard, as a lodge in a garden of cucumbers, as a besieged city. Except the Lord of hosts had left unto us a very small remnant, we should have been as Sodom, and we should have been like unto Gomorrah. Hear the Word of the Lord, ye rulers of Sodom; give ear unto the law of our God, ye people of Gomorrah. To what purpose is the multitude of your sacrifices unto me? saith the Lord: I am full of the burnt offerings of rams, and the fat of fed beasts; and I delight not in the blood of bullocks, or of lambs, or of he goats. When ye come to appear before me, who hath required this at your hand, to tread [trample] my courts? Bring no more vain oblations; incense is an abomination unto me; the new moons and Sabbaths, the calling of assemblies, I cannot away with; it is iniquity, even the solemn meeting. Your new moons and your appointed feasts my soul hateth: they are trouble unto me; I am weary to bear them. And when ye spread forth your hands, I will hide Mine eyes from you: yea, when ye make many prayers, I will not hear: your hands are full of blood.

God is clearly furious with His people at this point and indicts them with some serious charges. Among the many accusations made against them, the Lord accuses them of offering up the traditional ceremonial sacrifices and offerings at their celebrations, but their hearts were insincere and far from God. Israel's sacrifices were to be an outward sign of their inward faith in, love for and devotion to God; however, these outward signs became empty and meaningless because their hearts were full of sin and waywardness and they had no faith in their Maker. Essentially, they were simply going through the motions. The ultimate sacrifice that we as the church can bring to God is our bodies (our lives). Paul admonishes us in Romans 12:1, "...present your bodies a living sacrifice, holy, acceptable unto God, which is your reasonable service." Many in the church today have lost the true reverence of giving our lives to God in a way that is pleasing to Him. We have become ritualistic and routine in serving Him and lack the passion that He is calling for and that was eminent in the old church. Without regard for His sovereignty, we come to church willy-nilly as if we are doing God a favor by showing up on Sunday. Some of us are so heartless in our attitudes toward God that during praise and worship service (or devotion as some may call it), it is like pulling teeth for the Lord to get a praise out of us. This is why it takes a whole praise and worship team of cheerleaders to pump up this leprous church that does not show up for service with praise on their lips and worship in their bellies. Many of our services are either dead and dry or full of vibrant fleshly performances - and we call ourselves giving God the sacrifice of praise. According to this passage in Isaiah chapter one, God said, "Bring no more vain oblations..." He said, "Don't bring me any more junk praise, raggedy worship, and trashy lifestyles!"

Did you know that God does not accept everything we offer Him? Neither do you accept everything that is offered to you. It depends on what is offered to you, how it is offered, and who is offering it. If someone presented you dinner with spoiled chicken and rotten potatoes on a dirty plate with grimy silverware along with water in a muddy glass with debris and particles floating in it, you certainly would not accept this meal and would be quite offended at the offering. You would probably wonder what the person thought of you to present something so low grade to you. Well, this is how God feels about what we offer Him. In Malachi 1:6 - 9, God says,

> A son honors his father, and a servant his master. If I am a Father, where is the honor due Me? If I am a Master, where is the respect due Me?" says the Lord Almighty. "It is you, O priests, who show contempt for My name. But you ask, 'How have we shown contempt for Your name?' You place defiled food on My altar. But you ask, 'How have we defiled You?' By saying that the Lord's table is contemptible. When you bring blind animals for sacrifice, is that not wrong? When you sacrifice crippled or diseased animals, is that not wrong? Try offering them to your governor! Would he be pleased with you? Would he accept you?" says the Lord Almighty. "Now implore God to be gracious to us. With such offerings from your hands, will He accept you?" - says the Lord Almighty. (LASB)

The Word of the Lord instructed the priests to offer to God clean, undefiled food on the altar and animal sacrifices without blemish or defect. The Lord Jehovah was very particular about His offerings and His altar. However, Israel had degraded the Lord's altar by bringing and offering to Him defiled food and blind, crippled, and diseased animal sacrifices for God to accept. God was saying to Israel that they would not offer anything that filthy and degrading to their governor, and if they did, the governor certainly would not have accepted it. In today's church in general, we have brought ourselves to the Father in similar manner as living sacrifices (Romans 12:1) full of spots and blemishes. As done by the priests of Isaiah and Malachi's day, we constantly present ourselves to God wanting Him to accept and use us while we are miserably spiritually blind and can not see in the Spirit; crippled and unable to walk upright before God, and diseased with the plague of leprosy because of the flesh. Imagine Samuel (1 Samuel 9:9, 19) as a seer who could not see. Envision God giving Noah (Genesis 6:13 - 22) the plans to build the ark and he could not hear. Consider Elijah the prophet with no Word from the Lord in his mouth. (1 Kings 17:1 - 5) Sounds crazy? Well, it may sound crazy, but this is exactly what is happening in the church today. We have overseers who can not see or discern God at all, yet they desire to lead the people. My question is this: Where are you leading God's flock when you can not discern Him and do not know where you are going yourself? You need God's direction to lead God's people. A blind seer is a blemished sacrifice. We also have prophets and prophetesses with no true Word in their mouths; therefore they make up their own words to replace God's prophetic Word because they are spiritually deaf and can not hear God. A lying, spiritually deaf prophet that can not hear God is also a blemished sacrifice that is not accepted by God.

Instead of hearing and discerning God, we like Israel in Isaiah's day, generally do not wait to get instruction from the Lord on how we are to serve in His temple or kingdom, instead we come up with our own gatherings and meetings that God has not ordained or called. Remember, we talked about it before how we stay busy having conferences and programs just to say that we had our "5th Annual Choir Day" or our "35th Annual Women's Convention" but God never gets

126

the glory. Further, we are overloaded across the Body of Christ with conferences of every kind. God says in Isaiah 1:12 - 15, "When ye come to appear before me, who hath required this at your hand, to tread my courts?...the calling of assemblies, I cannot away with; it is iniquity, even the solemn meeting. Your new moons and your appointed feasts my soul hateth: they are trouble unto me; I am weary to bear them. And when ye spread forth your hands, I will hide Mine eyes from you: yea, when ye make many prayers, I will not hear: your hands are full of blood." Is God talking to you? Is He weary of your meetings? Has leprosy hit your conferences?

The Lord beckons Israel in Isaiah 1:16 - 27,

Wash you, make you clean; put away the evil of your doings from before mine eyes; cease to do evil; Learn to do well; seek judgment, relieve the oppressed, judge the fatherless, plead for the widow. Come now, and let us reason together, saith the Lord: though your sins be as scarlet, they shall be *white as snow*; though they be red like crimson, they shall be as wool. If ye be willing and obedient, ye shall eat the good of the land: But if ye refuse and rebel, ye shall be devoured with the sword: for the mouth of the Lord hath spoken it. How is the faithful city become an harlot! it is full of judgment; righteousness lodged in it; but now murderers. Thy silver is become dross, thy wine mixed with water: Thy princes are rebellious, and companions of thieves: every one loveth gifts, and followeth after rewards: they judge not the fatherless, neither doth the cause of the widow come unto them. Therefore saith the Lord, the Lord of hosts, the mighty One of Israel, Ah, I will ease me of mine adversaries, and avenge Me of

Mine enemies: And I will turn My hand upon thee and purely [thoroughly] purge away thy dross, and take away all thy tin: And I will restore thy judges as at the first, and thy counselors as at the beginning: afterward thou shalt be called, The city of *righteousness*, the faithful city. Zion shall be redeemed with judgment, and her converts with *righteousness*.

What a powerful representation of the fulfillment of Leviticus 13:12, 13 that says,

And if a leprosy break out abroad in the skin, and the leprosy cover all the skin of him that hath the plague from his head even to his foot, whereso-ever the priest looketh; Then the priest shall con-sider: and, behold, if the leprosy have covered all his flesh, he shall pronounce him clean that hath the plague: it is all turned white: he is clean.

Because leprosy has spread across the entire Body of Christ we have come to a major threshold in the Spirit. The church is at a powerful turning point in its history where the Lord is about to bring revival and the fire of God to wash us clean. Anytime God's people come to a place of complete disarray, sin, idolatry, waywardness, and dead works, the Spirit of the Lord sends a strong wind of refreshing to cleanse and renew His people. The Bible speaks of the *times of refreshing* in Acts 3:19 where Peter says, "Repent ye therefore, and be converted, that your sins may be blotted out, when the times of refreshing shall come from the pres-ence of the Lord..." Christendom has come to that set time as true repentance will usher in a real refreshing. The church has been so plagued by religiosity and the flesh to the point where another bruise from chastisement will do us absolutely no good because we have become seriously afflicted in our heads, wounded in our hearts, and bruised from head to foot. We are numb to chastisement. This is how we know and confirm prophetically that a tremendous shift in the Spirit is about to break forth. God is beckoning the church to come back to the altar and exchange our wounded Body for cleansing and healing. Since the whole Body is bruised and leprous from head to foot, then the whole Body must repent and return to the altar from head to foot - from pastors and leaders to pew members. Then God says to His people in Isaiah 1:18, "though your sins be as scarlet, they shall be *white as snow.*" God in this context is talking to those that already belong to Him - His own people. This altar call is for us, not the so-called unregenerate, unsaved sinners in the world. He goes on to promise to make us a city of *righteousness* robed in white, fine linen ready to meet our Maker and Father.

To the righteous who are a part of that small remnant spoken of in Isaiah 1:9, the Spirit of the Lord encourages your heart today to know that your prayers and fasting has not been in vain and gone unnoticed by God. It has been because of your sincere crying out, "Mercy!" before God on behalf of the people that His hand is now in the process of provoking a harvest of righteousness that will transform the leprous church. When you see that leprosy has broken out all across the Body, inflicting it from head to foot, then sense in the Spirit and hear the prophetic promise of God through His Word that the Body is on its way to becoming white as snow by the cleansing of the blood. Be encouraged and know that true redemption, deliverance and cleansing draweth nigh (Luke 21:28) and are at the door, because Leviticus 13:13 prophesies that the fully leprous man shall be pronounced clean.

Chapter 9

Stop The Plague!

Stop The Plague!
~ Cleansing The Leprous House ~

---

*F*rom the revelation and illumination that God unveiled
to us in the chapters of this book, we clearly see the
true effects and detriment of the spread of the plague of leprosy in the life of an individual, a church or a ministry. We
now recognize through the Word of truth what it is that has
actually been affecting the church for quite some time and
how far it has progressed. Therefore, it is urgent that we all
endeavor to quench the spread of this contagion, beginning
with a personal internal check on ourselves in order to crucify the flesh. Although many of us have been operating
according to our own carnality, the fact that this Word is
being released to the Body of Christ during the 21st century
demonstrates the love of God toward His people and the
plan of God to cleanse and prepare us for this great end-time
move of God that is about to break forth and usher in the
return of the Lord Jesus. Divine illumination now makes you
responsible and accountable to take this Word and apply it
as the treatment against leprosy and stop the plague!

In scripture, being inflicted with leprosy did not have to
constitute an automatic death sentence. The leper or the leprous house could be cleansed and healed. God gave Moses

specific instructions on how to go about cleansing the leprous house, the details of which are too immense to deal with in the context of this book. Therefore, prepare your heart for the next dimension of revelation destined to take you to even higher heights and deeper depths on your journey to a powerful place in God through volume two of ***"Leprosy In The Church: Cleansing The Leprous House."***

"Leprosy In The Church" is not only purposed to identify the symptoms that prove and diagnose the overall condition of the church, but it is intended to be a tool and a measure by which you can generally determine how healthy you are spiritually. Therefore, a Spiritual Wellness Check is made available for you in the following section of this book to allow you to measure yourself by the Word and begin steps toward purification and another dimension in the Holy Spirit.

SPIRITUAL WELLNESS CHECK

Overview of
~ Spiritual Wellness Check ~

*E*ssentially every segment of society has a means by which to determine how well it is operating or functioning. Major corporations have various measures to determine overall company performance via sales performance records, stock market tracking, productivity reports to monitor how well they manufacture products without defects, etc. They even analyze how their employees function through performance appraisals to review how effective they are in accomplishing their day-to-day tasks. Pharmaceutical companies conduct clinical studies to measure how well a research drug performs on people with certain diseases before releasing the medicine to the public. If it does not work well based on the results of the studies, then they either discontinue the research or try to improve the drug by modifying how it is made. Automobile insurance companies monitor closely the number of points that accumulate on your driving record so that they can significantly increase your insurance rates. Every measure that is assessed is for the purpose of making decisions on whether to continue in the current direction or to make adjustments for a better outcome.

The church is one of the very few institutions that makes little or no attempt to use analytical measures to assess the health of our churches, ministries and even personal lives based on a common standard - the Word of God. In other words, the same measure that is applied to one applies to all. In the kingdom of God, things are approached in a very nebulous and grayscale manner, and we often go by our feelings and intuition versus real founded, hardcore metrics to tell us where we are, where God wants us to be, and how we can bridge the gap between the two. John gives an account of his encounter with an angel sent from God in Revelation 11:1 where he says,

> And there was given me a reed like unto a rod: and the angel stood, saying, Rise, and measure the temple of God, and the altar, and them that worship therein.

John speaks of how during the vision that the Spirit of the Lord had revealed to him concerning the end time, the angel that was sent to bring him this revelation gave him a measuring reed or rod that he was to use to measure the temple, the altar and the worshippers or people of God in the temple. He was to measure each of these to determine if they were built according to God's pattern and instruction. Some have interpreted that the Lord sent the angel to instruct John to number the people to determine how many people were in the temple. However, Ezekiel 40:3 speaks of the vision God gave the prophet Ezekiel of a man with a measuring reed that was used to measure different areas of the temple in order to compare them against the original dimensions that God had instructed they be made according to His Word in the book of Exodus. So, in essence, the measuring reed symbolized the Word of God and was the comparison used to determine whether or not what God spoke had been established. Jesus said in Matthew 7:2,

For with what judgment ye judge, ye shall be judged: and with what measure ye mete, it shall be measured to you again.

The word *mete* translates from the Greek word *metreo* which means to measure or to determine size or stature by a fixed standard or rule. In other words, Jesus was teaching that whatever standard or rule you size up someone else against will be the same that is used against you. Then Paul later speaks about the five-fold ministry offices and says that they are given by God to the church for the following purpose as described in Ephesians 4:12 -13,

For the perfecting of the saints, for the work of the ministry, for the edifying of the Body of Christ: Till we all come in the unity of the faith, and of the knowledge of the Son of God, unto a perfect man, unto the measure of the stature of the fullness of Christ...

Paul is saying that one of the purposes of the offices of the apostles, prophets, evangelists, pastors and teachers is to perfect or mature the saints until we reach the full measure established by Christ Jesus who is the rule or the standard for all that is holy. Jesus said in John 14:6, "...I am the Way, the Truth and the Life..." and goes on to pray to the Father regarding the disciples in John 17:17 where He says, "Sanctify them through Thy truth: Thy Word is Truth." Therefore, since Jesus is the Truth and the Word of the Father is the Truth, then that makes Jesus equivalent to the Word. So this means that when we are measured against Jesus, then we are measured against the Word of God which is the reed spoken of in Revelation 11:1. The question then becomes this: Do we measure up to the standard of holiness established by the Lord Jesus through His

Word or have we simply compared ourselves to each other which the scriptures speak against? In fact, Paul says in 2 Corinthians 10:12,

> We do not dare to classify or compare ourselves with those who commend themselves. When they measure themselves by themselves and compare themselves with themselves, they are not wise. (LASB)

Here Paul confirms that to measure and compare ourselves with others is not wise, but we must judge ourselves against the Word of God to see how we really measure up against the true Gold Standard.

The reason I mention all of this is because the Lord spoke to me back in May of 2002 and told me to *"measure the people."* I was driving in my car at the time He lifted this up to me. He then took me to Revelation 11:1 and gave me an assignment to provide calculated measures by which the people of God can analyze their lives based on and against the Word of God. All throughout my professional career, I have applied measures and have even created analytical metrics in the work I have done from research chemical engineering to corporate strategy consulting. For seven and a half years I worked for Merck & Co., Inc., a top global pharmaceutical company, as a Research Chemical Engineer co-inventing prescription drugs, one of which was prescribed to former basketball star Magic Johnson. Then after earning a MBA from the Wharton graduate school of business where I learned to develop measures on a corporate or company scale, I joined PricewaterhouseCoopers as an executive management consultant assisting CEO's, presidents, vice presidents and other senior managers to assess the health of their organizations and to develop business strategies for future visioning. In this position, I also created and applied measures or metrics to analyze the company's performance against a set of standards. Therefore, I have a strong analytical background.

At the time I heard God instruct me to measure the people, the Spirit of the Lord also spoke saying, *"Now take the skills you have developed in Corporate America and use them to help My people."* I was still a consultant at PricewaterhouseCoopers at that time and did not know how all this would unfold. All I knew was that I heard the voice of God. So I immediately began to develop analytical measures for the people of God. It is important to note that during the Lord's discourse with me about the church and this aspect of my life's assignment to help build up the church, I sensed such a strong, overwhelmingly love from the heart of God for His people to the degree that it brought me to tears. Then I heard Him say, *"I am using every avenue in these last days to clean up my church and bring them closer to Me."* What a loving God we serve!

Therefore, the Lord instructed me to transfer my professional skills that I developed and applied in Corporate America and likewise apply them in the church as a supplement and a tool for the saints to determine where we are in our walk with God and how far we are from the mark and measure set by the example and standard of Jesus Christ through His Word. Because God loves us so much and wants us to get it right with Him, He has provided for us another avenue through this assessment and others He has given me to make available for the Body of Christ which are tailored for churches and ministries to more specifically measure their leadership, music ministries, and those with evangelical callings - prophets, evangelists, etc. (For more information, contact Morrison Ministries.) It is high time for us to really see how far we are from the measure of the fullness of Christ and begin to rid ourselves of the leprosy that has plagued and spread in the church.

The following now provides you with instructions on how to conduct your Spiritual Wellness Check to generally determine how spiritually healthy you are.

~ Spiritual Wellness Check ~

*T*his Spiritual Wellness Check is Biblically based and designed to provide you with a general diagnosis and *measure* of how spiritually healthy you are. In order for you to benefit from this assessment, it is imperative that you be completely honest with yourself and provide answers that accurately reflect your true character. Again, score yourself honestly. One of the worst things that we can do is lie to ourselves, and if we want to take steps toward mounting to a higher place in God, we must no longer deceive ourselves but be truthful by using the mirror of the Word to examine our own hearts.

Therefore, please provide your most candidate and honest answers to the questions starting on the following page using a scale of 1 - 5 with one being the lowest score and five being the highest. Place your answer or score in the box in the right hand column. Once you have completed all 100 questions, calculate your total score at the end of the wellness check and place your total score in the box provided. Once you have totaled your score, your Spiritual Wellness Results can be found immediately following the diagnostic. Match your score with the appropriate assessment of how spiritually healthy you are and this is your general measure of spiritual health according to the Word of God.

Scriptural medicine is also provided at the end of this wellness check based on your spiritual condition to help point you in the right direction towards treatment which will mount you to greater empowerment in the Spirit. As you grow in God and become more purified, I highly recommend that you take this assessment over and over again as you continue to cleanse yourself by the Word. Further, as you become more transformed by the Spirit to the image of Christ, you will have a cleaner bill of spiritual health which will be reflected in the results of your Spiritual Wellness Check.

DISCLAIMER: Although this diagnostic has been tested for soundness before releasing it in this book, it is not to be taken as professional counseling or psychological advice. It is neither intended to be a replacement for spiritual leadership in your church or ministry, but is purposed to be a supplement and a tool for you to use in analyzing your life against the Word of God. Once you have completed this diagnostic, consult with the Lord and with your spiritual leader to determine next steps for your next dimension to which this Word once received and applied will take you in your journey to righteousness, holiness and power.

~ Spiritual Wellness Check ~

0 - Strongly Disagree	1 - Disagree	2 - Somewhat	3 - Agree
	4 - Strongly Agree		

	Questions	Score
1.	My desire for recognition and position is the main reason I do what I do in church or ministry.	0
2.	I could serve God better if I had more money.	0
3.	I like to control people's lives.	1
4.	I don't really think about the coming of the Lord (rapture) all that much.	2
5.	Most of my friends are unsaved because I really don't get along all that well with people in the church.	0
6.	If I wasn't saved and could get away with it, there are some people I would wipe off the face of the earth.	1
7.	When I go to church or other ministry meetings, I often desire for someone to prophesy to me personally.	1
8.	I love to or wish I could prophesy because it seems that people like to receive prophetic Words from God.	1
9.	When I see people sinning or know that they have sin in their lives in the church, I don't say anything to them because that is between them and God.	2
10.	It does not really matter that the church is run exactly the way the Bible says, as long as it functions okay and the people seem happy, then that is okay.	1
11.	It is impossible to live exactly the way the Bible or God commands these days because it takes too much in such a sinful world.	2

12.	There is someone that I can think of right now who I am jealous of.	2
13.	People always tell me how great the work I do in the kingdom is and that makes me feel really good.	1
14.	I use manipulative methods to get people to do what I want them to do.	0
15.	To tell a little white lie is okay, as long as you are not hurting anybody and it is for a good reason.	2
16.	I love to be in charge all the time.	0
17.	My pastor, parents, or other leader in my life is the reason I have not gotten to the place that God wants me.	0
18.	It is hard for me to follow someone else's lead because I often find things wrong with how other people do things and I often find a better way to get things done.	0
19.	If things are not done my way, then I often withdraw from what is going on and do not participate because God is not the author of confusion.	1
20.	Although I mean well, many things I do often cause division or trouble around me - whether at church, at work or at home.	2
21.	I try to get close to people that I know are popular.	1
22.	I'd rather listen to preaching or music tapes than read the Bible.	0
23.	If my pastor, bishop or other spiritual leader were really in the Spirit, then he/she would recognize the gift of God in me.	3 2
24.	I am more anointed than people realize.	1
25.	Because I can't understand the scriptures, I don't read the Bible much because it is like I'm reading a foreign language.	0 1
26.	God is not really concerned about the little things we do like exaggerating on your taxes or envying someone.	0

27.	If someone does something against me, I make it my business to get back at them in some way no matter how long it takes me to do it.	6
28.	Being on time for church is not important.	6
29.	I do the things I do in the church or ministry with the aim to please the pastor or ministry leader rather than God.	0
30.	Every time I hear a sermon preached, I can think of someone else that needs to hear that particular message more than me.	1
31.	I don't really have a lot of faults.	0
32.	There is a position (or positions) in church or ministry that someone else is currently functioning in that I know belongs to me. Once they are removed then I will be able to take my rightful place.	
33.	I do not fast or consecrate often.	3
34.	I have no clue about what God called me to do.	2
35.	When I go to church, I need the choir or music ministry to lift up my spirit.	1
36.	I often become very moody and difficult to be around.	1
37.	I can not say that I remember God telling me to do what I am doing right now in the kingdom.	
38.	It is not important to have a pastor or someone to shepherd over me because these days all pastors want is your money.	
39.	I don't need a church home because I can visit churches and watch Christian television to supply my spiritual needs.	
40.	I am late when I go to church.	
41.	There is a reason why I behave the way I do and people simply need to understand that I have been through a lot in my life.	

42. It is easier to please people than it is to please God; so I try my best to make sure that people are happy with what I do because a lot of times I don't know what God wants anyway.	
43. I feel that if I don't function in my position in church or ministry, then the services will not be what they should be.	
44. It makes me feel good to know that my position, gift or talent is greatly needed in the church and if I don't show up things don't go right.	
45. Other people's preaching often bores me if it is not someone I like.	
46. I try as much as I can to make sure that everyone around me likes me.	
47. I don't think that you should ever cut people off and remove them out of your life in the church because you don't know what God could be using you to do in their lives.	
48. When I attend a special ministry event (e.g. conference, revival, etc.) and I am not seated where I think I should be seated based on my title, position, or personal desire, then I get angry and just may leave.	
49. If ever I have to sit in the overflow room for a service, then I just leave and go home because overflow rooms are uncomfortable and is not like actually being in the main auditorium or sanctuary where the service is being held.	
50. I don't need anybody to tell me anything because I hear directly from God on my own.	
51. When I see people doing things in church, I always find fault in some way and feel that I can do better. I am just analytical like that.	
52. I talk about people in a bad way.	
53. I am involved in gossip and do get together with others whether by phone or over dinner to discuss what I don't like about people.	

54. I compliment people to make them feel good when I don't really mean what I'm saying.	
55. I go along with the crowd so that I will not be the only one not in agreement with everybody else. It's easier that way.	
56. It is okay to hate someone as long as you don't show it and they don't know it.	
57. I must admit that I do have a problem with jealousy and am jealous of someone.	
58. I only deal with people like me.	
59. People from some other races bother me, and I have a problem really accepting certain ethnic groups.	
60. I don't say this openly to people, but on the inside, I feel that my race or ethnic group is better than any other.	
61. If two people were stranded on the street and one of them was of my race and the other was not, and I could only help one person, I would feel obligated without question to help my own race.	
62. When people don't do things the way I think they should be done, I usually stop dealing with them; or if a situation is run in a way I don't think it should be, then I usually do not participate.	
63. I am afraid to tell people the truth about themselves because I don't want to hurt anyone's feelings.	
64. It does not matter how you treat people, as long as you get the will of God done.	
65. If I don't like someone, then I try to ruin their reputation by turning others against them.	
66. I tear people down when they do things against me.	
67. My church, ministry, auxiliary, etc. is so warm and friendly that we allow anyone to participate as long as they are saved.	

68. When things go right under my leadership, I feel really good about it and anticipate people's compliments.	
69. I become discouraged and begin to question myself if I'm not complimented after I preach, prophesy, sing, usher, cook for a ministry event, or serve otherwise in ministry.	
70. I have a problem with sincerely asking for forgiveness when I have wronged someone.	
71. There is someone I love more than God.	
72. I get so busy that I can not pray everyday.	
73. People should feel privileged to serve in my church, ministry, auxiliary, on my team, or be my friend, etc. because of who I am in God.	
74. Excellence is not important as long as you get the job done.	
75. I compare myself to others in the church either in my mind or while talking with someone else. This helps me to determine how good I am at what I do.	
76. When I see people who consult God in everything they do, I really feel it does not take all that.	
77. When hardship and loss of personal comfort comes into my life, I get mad with God.	
78. When I have an ought against someone, I feel it is better to just keep it inside and not cause any conflict by bringing it up with them.	
79. I listen to secular music that contains vulgarity and/or sexual connotations.	
80. I smoke cigarettes.	
81. I still do drugs (marijuana, cocaine, crack, heroine, etc.)	
82. Holiness is something the old sanctified church always preached but is not important today.	

83. I don't accept when people point out bad things about me.	
84. I get offended when someone highlights my faults; so I begin to highlight theirs.	
85. I make excuses for my mistakes and feel that people should understand.	
86. When I try to get my point across, I will keep pushing till the person is won over to my way of thinking because I feel that I am usually always right.	
87. I don't think it is important to work in the church as long as you come to church every Sunday.	
88. I come to church when I can but it does not matter if I'm not there because no one will miss me since I don't do much (or anything) or what I do is not important.	
89. The main reason I am faithful to or come to church is so that my pastor, mother, spouse or someone else won't get mad at me. Otherwise, I would not come as much or at all.	
90. Preaching normally bores me and I usually get nothing out of the message.	
91. I think that the best part of the service is when the praise and worship team and/or the choir sing. When it is time for the sermon, I become disinterested and really want to leave at that point.	
92. When I am angry or worried, I don't feel like worshipping.	
93. I would rather dance and shout than worship.	
94. I feel that worship is not important to me.	
95. I have been a member of 3 or more churches in the last 3 to 5 years.	
96. When I am prophesying but don't really know what God is saying, I make up something so that I won't be embarrassed or to make the person feel good about what I am saying.	

97. I do not pay my tithes.	
98. When I prophesy or give a message to people from the Lord (preaching, prophesying, etc.), the message is usually always good and encouraging and people get excited about what I tell them.	
99. I can not take criticism without being sensitive, defensive, and confrontational.	
100. I think that worldly wisdom works better than Biblical principles in today's church and society.	
TOTAL SCORE	

0 - Strongly Disagree   1 - Disagree   2 - Somewhat   3 - Agree

4 - Strongly Agree

~ Spiritual Wellness Results ~ (Leprosy Factor)	
Total Score	**Diagnosis: How Spiritually Healthy Are You?**
301 - 400	**SERIOUSLY, CHRONICALLY LEPROUS.** You have the worst case of spiritual leprosy and are seriously spotted by the flesh. Carnality has set you on a course of self-righteousness and pride that has placed you far off track with God. You tend to be high-minded and full of yourself, doing things according to your own will instead of the will of God. You are very likely a jealous, malicious, deceptive person who manipulates others to achieve your own goals and you have a tendency not to be very truthful. You tend to love to control others, and will close yourself off from those that do not do what you say. If you are not the one spearheading events or situations, then you tend not to fully support the work of the Lord through others. It is very likely that you reject when others point out your faults because it is hard for you to see yourself the way you really are. You have refused and rejected the truth about yourself; therefore you tend to make enemies out of those who do not agree with your ways and you love flattery that swells your flesh. Further, you have a problem with church leadership, find it difficult to submit to God's delegated authority, and have your own agenda and are quite competitive. In fact, you may be currently walking in pure rebellion which the Bible says is as the sin of witchcraft (1 Samuel 15:23). People scoring in this category include those who typically harbor spirits of witchcraft and divination and operate under familiar spirits. These are your church propheliars, lying evangelists, controlling ministers and pastors, or others who have a "cliquish" group within the church who fight against spiritual leadership, etc. Scoring in this category indicates that you are very likely a thorn to the kingdom of God and work against the will and purpose of the Lord within church ministry. It is an emergency in the Spirit that you apply the strong medicine of the Word of the

301 - 400 (cont.)	Lord Jesus to stop this serious plague that has hit your heart. However, do not be discouraged to find out how spiritually unhealthy you are. This is the purpose for the wellness check so that you can come out of darkness and become aware of your condition which the enemy has tried to hide from you possibly for a long time. Take this diagnosis as God's means of putting you on your journey to inner healing and empowerment in Christ and know that God loves you enough to turn the light on your true condition in order to heal your heart. Therefore, it is strongly recommended that you make a serious spiritual adjustment in your walk with God and approach to serving in the church. You must die to your flesh and your own will, remove the filthy garments of self-righteousness, pride and rebellion, wash yourself with the Word of God, come out of darkness and begin to walk in the light. You can start to do this by applying the scriptural medicine provided below along with other scriptures you may reference. Also go back to those passages in this book that highlighted your leprous spots and use the scripture references provided there as well. Next, consult with the Lord and your spiritual leader (along with other truly God-fearing people) on next steps for your next dimension in God. *SCRIPTURAL MEDICINE:* 2 Chronicles 7:14; Romans 1:18 - 32, 6:1 - 23; 12:1; Galatians chapter 5, Isaiah 1:16 - 20; 2 Corinthians 7:1; 2 Peter chapter 2; 1 John 1:5 - 10; Ephesians 4:17 - 32, 5:1 - 20, 27; John 1:1, 4, 5, 9; 8:12; Philippians 4:13. [This is just a start. God will unfold many other scriptures as you study His Word.]
201 - 300	<u>VERY LEPROUS.</u> You are very leprous and spotted by the flesh in many ways. You possess many of the characteristics of the seriously, chronically leprous person, but to a lesser degree of manifestation. Although you do not have the worst case of spiritual leprosy, your condition does not lag far behind the worst case. You tend to be somewhat high-minded, self-willed and allow your carnal nature to dictate what you do in the kingdom of God. Carnality has set you on a course of self-righteousness and pride that has placed you off track with God. You tend to function according to your own will instead of the will of God. You also deal with jealousy, malice, and use deceptive tactics at times when it is convenient for you to achieve your own goals. You like to have things to go your way and also appreciate having a heavy influence on others to the point of control.

201 - 300 (cont.)	Typically when there is a battle between your flesh and the Spirit of God, your flesh wins and you go along with what is easiest to satisfy your own carnal desires. To a spiritually unhealthy degree, your desire for advancement in the church and ministry is based on natural abilities and not completely on divine timing and ordered steps. (Psalm 37:23). You must reassess the motives behind why you serve in the kingdom and bring them in alignment with the Word of God. When you do this, you will realize a major shift in your understanding of divine timing and have the proper perspective on where true spiritual promotion comes from (Psalm 75:6, 7). You have a level of tenderness in your heart toward God, but have not allow that soft-spot for the Lord to produce obedience due to your carnal nature. People scoring in this category may be involved with the work of the Lord, but also create stumbling blocks for other leaders by gossip, backbiting and chatter. It is very likely that you too, like the seriously leprous, reject when others point out your faults because it is hard for you to see yourself the way you really are. Although you may give some thought to the truth that others speak concerning your faults, you tend to more quickly refuse and reject the truth about yourself when it is difficult to accept. You distance yourself from those who do not agree with your ways and gravitate to flattery that swells your flesh. You tend to have strong issues with church leadership and find it difficult to submit to God's delegated authority; but you may put on the façade that you are in agreement when in fact you strongly oppose, while concurrently trying to undermine the work of the Lord with your gossip. You can be quite deceptive at times and look for opportunities to make inroads for yourself in church or ministry. In fact, you may be currently walking in rebellion which the Bible says is as the sin of witchcraft (1 Samuel 15:23). People scoring in this category also (as with the seriously, chronically leprous) include those who are typical targets for spirits of witchcraft and divination and familiar spirits. These are your church propheliars, lying evangelists, controlling ministers and pastors, or others who have a "cliquish" group within the church who fight against spiritual leadership, etc., but are not as overt as the seriously, chronically leprous. Scoring in this category indicates that you are very likely one who causes schisms and division in the kingdom of God and work against the will and purpose of the Lord within church ministry. It is an urgent in the Spirit that you apply the strong medicine of

201 - 300 (cont.)	the Word of the Lord Jesus to stop this serious plague that has hit your heart. However, do not be discouraged to find out how spiritually unhealthy you are. This is the purpose for the wellness check so that you can come out of darkness and become aware of your condition which the enemy has tried to hide from you possibly for a long time. Take this diagnosis as God's means of putting you on your journey to inner healing and empowerment in Christ and know that God loves you enough to turn the light on your true condition in order to heal your heart. Therefore, it is strongly recommended that you make a serious spiritual adjustment in your walk with God and approach to serving in the church. You must die to your flesh and your own will, remove the filthy garments of self-righteousness, pride and rebellion, wash yourself with the Word of God, come out of darkness and begin to walk in the light. You can start to do this by applying the scriptural medicine provided below along with other scriptures you may reference. Also go back to those passages in this book that highlighted your leprous spots and use the scripture references provided there as well. Next, consult with the Lord and your spiritual leader (along with other truly God-fearing people) on next steps for your next dimension in God. **SCRIPTURAL MEDICINE:** 2 Chronicles 7:14; Romans 1:18 - 32, 6:1 - 23; 12:1; Galatians chapter 5, Isaiah 1:16 - 20; 2 Corinthians 7:1; 2 Peter chapter 2; 1 John 1:5 - 10; Ephesians 4:17 - 32, 5:1 - 20, 27; John 1:1, 4, 5, 9; 8:12; Philippians 4:13. [This is just a start. God will unfold many other scriptures as you study His Word.]
101 - 200	**MODERATELY SPOTTED WITH LEPROSY.** You are somewhat spotted with leprous ways. You tend to straddle the fence and can be quite double-minded in your approach to serving God. Your general desire is to do what is right and to walk upright before God, but when tribulation hits in your life, you tend to allow circumstances to cause you to fall from your place in God. Your heart responds to the Word of God when it is comfortable and convenient. You tend to sometimes be indifferent about the work of the Lord when you do not see the purpose for why things are done in the church. You tend to try to clean up your life when the Word of the Lord highlights your sins. Your general desire is to please the Lord and you would obey Him more if you had good solid instruction on how to serve Him based on the Word of God. There are certain things you are holding on to that have spotted your heart and that God is

**101 - 200
(cont.)**

requiring you to let go of because they are the stumbling blocks to your next dimension in Him. However, you have not submitted these areas and have remained in a state of flux in the Spirit. Do not allow the fact that you may generally be a "nice person" to cause you to believe that your walk with God is leprosy free. People scoring in this category tend to be spotted with things like fear, depression, confusion, low self worth, rejection, paranoia, etc. because the enemy knows the power of that will be released in your life once you begin cleansing the leprous spots on your garments. The people around you may tend to cause you to swing from one side of the pendulum to the other when it comes to spiritual stability; therefore, you must cleanse your circle of company. You tend to shy away from trouble and may not often be in the midst of confusion. You have a decent passion for the things of God and desire to serve Him on a greater level. You tend, however, to struggle with what your true purpose, calling and destiny are in the kingdom. Otherwise, you function in a Christ-minded manner which serves you better. It is recommended that you begin to bring your spirit into complete alignment with God You can tend to be double-minded and lukewarm at times and must establish a steady walk with God. As you cleanse your heart with the washing of the water by the Word of God, you will find many things unfold in your life that have previously been held up.

You must continue to die to your flesh and your own will, washing yourself with the Word of God, so that you can walk in a greater manifestation of the light of God. You can start to do this by applying the scriptural medicine provided below along with other scriptures you may reference. Also go back to those passages in this book that highlighted your leprous spots and use the scripture references provided there as well. Next, consult with the Lord and your spiritual leader (along with other truly God-fearing people) on next steps for your next dimension in God.

SCRIPTURAL MEDICINE: 1 Kings 18:21; James 1:8; 4:8; 2 Chronicles 7:14; Romans 1:18 - 32, 6:1 - 23; 12:1; Galatians chapter 5, Isaiah 1:16 - 20; 1 Corinthians 5:6; 15:58; 2 Corinthians 7:1; 2 Peter chapter 2; 1 John 1:5 - 10; Ephesians 4:17 - 32, 5:1 - 20, 27; John 1:1, 4, 5, 9; 8:12; Philippians 4:13. [This is just a start. God will unfold many other scriptures as you study His Word.]

0 - 100	**SPARSELY LEPROUS** You essentially have a clean bill of spiritual health and are definitely a model of a Christ-minded believer. You take this spiritual death walk seriously and always seek to go deeper in God and please Him on a greater level. You should be commended for your walk with God and for endeavoring to constantly bring your life into alignment with the His divine Word. Jesus told His disciples, "...ye are clean, but not all." (John 13:10b), implying that there were those of His disciples who were and some who were not clean. You are generally one of His clean disciples. You have several followers that desire to mimic your walk in God, seeking after the benefits of your purification but not desiring the crucifixion that comes along with achieving this level of good spiritual health. You have a healthy understanding that promotion comes from the Lord and that the divine timing of God seldom reflects man's timing and the flawed human will. You generally tend to want only what the Lord has designed for your life. Your main challenge at times is knowing what the will of God is; once you hear Him, you tend to obey quickly. You try earnestly to distinguish the difference between your will and the will of God and do attempt to remove spots from your garments as they appear. It is recommended that you become a leader in championing others to transform their thinking by the Word of God and be an example (Philippians 3:17) for others to follow hard after the Almighty. God desires to use you as a Nathan in the church. The enemy would love to cause you to compromise, not with what the church considers to be major sins like murder, drug addiction, adultery, etc., but he seeks to cause you to stumble by your not hearing and obeying the voice of God when He gives you instruction for an assignment. Be careful of the little leaven that leavens the lump and the small foxes that spoil the vine. Make sure you guard your heart against self-righteousness, false humility, and the flattery and vain accolades of others as these are the kinds of sparse spots that affect people who score in this category. Continue to guard and keep your garments according to Revelation 16:15. Apply the scriptural medicine provided below along with other scriptures you may reference to maintain your spiritual health and to cleanse you from the sparse spots on your garments. Also go back to those passages in this book that highlighted your leprous blemishes and use the scripture references provided there as well.

0 - 100 (cont.)	Next, consult with the Lord and your spiritual leader (along with other truly God-fearing people) on next steps for your next dimension in God. **SCRIPTURAL MEDICINE:** Ecclesiastes 9:8; 1 Kings 8:22 - 61; Song of Solomon 2:15; Isaiah 64:6; Revelation 7:13, 14; 16:15; Luke 13:35; Colossians 2:4; Romans 15:1; Luke 22:32; 1 Corinthians 5:6; Ephesians 5:27. [This is just a start. God will unfold many other scriptures as you study His Word.]

~ ABOUT THE AUTHOR ~

*M*arcia Morrison has been serving the Lord for over 30 years. She is the president and founder of Morrison Ministries, a multi-faceted ministry wherein she operates out of the prophetic office and functions as an author, conference speaker, Bible instructor, consultant, revivalist, and psalmist. She develops books and other training materials to assist in providing sound Biblical teaching and guidance for the 21st century Church. She also walks under the spiritual covering and guidance of her father Suffragan Bishop Lawrence E. Brown, Sr. of the Pentecostal Assemblies of the World (PAW) in St. Louis, MO. As Morrison Ministries is based in New Jersey, Bishop George & Pastor Mary Searight and the Abundant Life Family Worship Church serve as the resident covering for Marcia's family and ministry.

Marcia holds a Master of Business Administration (MBA) from the Wharton School of the University of Pennsylvania and a B.S. in Chemical Engineering from Washington University in St. Louis. She has performed research to co-invent new medicines including an AIDS therapy. She was awarded The Wharton School's Howard E. Mitchell Fellowship and the Shils/Zeidman Entrepreneurial Scholarship (first two-time recipient in history of school). Prior to being called into full time ministry, Marcia was most recently employed with PricewaterhouseCoopers as a Pharmaceutical Consultant, developing competitive business strategies for CEOs, presidents, and vice presidents of top pharmaceutical companies such as Merck, Bristol Myers, Johnson & Johnson, etc. She has co-authored an article in the pharmaceutical industry magazine *"American Pharmaceutical Outsourcing"* and was invited to be a regular contributor to the publication.

Widowed in 2002 for the second time by the passing of her second deceased husband, the late Seth Morrison, Marcia bears a tenacious resilience against the perils of life through the power of the Spirit. She was honored by God for four years to have been married to and have shared a family and ministry with the late Seth Morrison, an anointed minstrel and organist who was highly dedicated to the work of the music ministry. The Lord called him to lay down his armor and rest from his labor on December 9, 2002. In honor and memory of her husband, she has founded the Minstrel Seth Morrison Scholarship Foundation to provide financial awards to assist and encourage musicians around the world. Marcia is also the blessed mother of two beautiful daughters, Chauncey Ciera and baby Mikailah Star, whom she nurtures and instructs in the admonition of the Lord. Whether raising her children, preaching the gospel, ministering in song, or spear heading organizations, Christ is the center of her every endeavor; and her sole desire is to be a servant vigilant for the Master's use.

For information on other ministry products (development materials, tapes, videos, etc.) of Marcia Morrison or to request her for a ministry event, please contact:

Morrison Ministries
P.O. Box 3868
Trenton, NJ 08629
(732) 940-3787 - phone
(609) 587-7653 - fax
E-mail: morrisonministry@aol.com
Website: www.morrisonministries.com

Printed in the United States
31776LVS00001B/139-186